BREAKING PHILOSOPHY

Timeless Wisdom Explained With Real Life Situations

DANIEL CHECHICK

Copyright © 2024
DANIEL CHECHICK
BREAKING PHILOSOPHY
Timeless Wisdom Explained With Real Life Situations
All rights reserved.

No part of this publication may be reproduced, distributed, or transmitted in any form or by any means, including photocopying, recording, or other electronic or mechanical methods, without the prior written permission of the author, except in the case of brief quotations embodied in critical reviews and certain other non-commercial uses permitted by copyright law.

DANIEL CHECHICK

Printed Worldwide
First Printing 2024
First Edition 2024

10 9 8 7 6 5 4 3 2 1

BREAKING PHILOSOPHY

Table of Contents

Introduction 1
Absolutism 3
Absurdism 5
Agnosticism 7
Aestheticism 9
Analytic Philosophy 11
Anarchism 13
Anti-realism 15
Aristotelianism 17
Asceticism 19
Atheological 21
Authenticity 24
Autonomism 26
Behaviorism 28
Bioethics 30
Cameralism 32
Casuistry 34
Cognitive relativism 36
Constructivism 38
Continental philosophy 40
Critical realism 42
Cultural determinism 44
Cultural Relativism 46
Cynicism 48
Daoism 50
Deconstructionism 52
Deep Ecology 55
Determinism 57
Digital Philosophy 59
Ecological Rationality 61
Emergentism 63
Epistemic Humility 65
Epistemic Injustice 67

Eclecticism	69
Egoism	71
Environmentalism	72
Equivocation	74
Eudaimonia	77
Evolutionary ethics	80
Existential Phenomenology	83
Existential Nihilism	85
Empiricism	87
Epicureanism	89
Existentialism	91
Foundationalism	94
Functionalism	96
Hedonism	98
Hegelian dialectic	100
Hermeneutic	103
Heterophenomenology	105
Historical materialism	107
Holism	109
Humanism	111
Hylomorphism	113
Imperative	115
Ideal Observer Theory	118
Idealism	120
Individualism	122
Indeterminacy	124
Inductive reasoning	127
Ineffability	130
Infinite regress	133
Inherence	135
Instrumentalism	137
Intension	139
Intersubjective	141
Intuitionism	143
Irrealism	145
Karma	148

Materialism	150
Machiavellianism	152
Necessitarianism	154
Neo-Kantianism	156
Nihilism	159
Objectivism	162
Panpsychism	164
Phenomenology	167
Postmodernism	169
Pantheism	171
Poststructuralism	173
Platonism	175
Pragmatism	177
Predestination	180
Pre-Socratic philosophy	182
Process Theology	185
Quietism	187
Rationalism	189
Realism	191
Relativism	193
Rhetoric	196
Sartrean Existentialism	200
Scientism	202
Skepticism	204
Solipsism	206
Sophism	208
Stoicism	211
Structuralism	214
Social contract theory	217
Structural Functionalism	220
Subjectivism	223
Transcendentalism	226
Further Readings	230

Introduction

In our hectic daily lives, we often find ourselves grappling with questions about the meaning of existence, our purpose, and the nature of reality. It's in these moments of introspection that the timeless wisdom of philosophy becomes a guiding light. In the book I have written, I aim to explain a droplet of the vast ocean of knowledge that philosophy contains.

As you embark on this exploration, you will learn about absurdism, existentialism, nihilism, stoicism, pragmatism, transcendentalism, and many more. But fear not, for I won't delve into the abstract and esoteric without a compass. Instead, I have drawn parallels between these philosophical concepts and our daily lives, weaving together insights that are as practical as they are profound.

Just as the ancient philosophers sought to make sense of the world around them, you too will uncover the relevance of their ideas in the context of modern existence. Whether you're grappling with the absurdities of life, seeking meaning in a seemingly indifferent universe, or striving for inner peace, this book offers a bridge between the ivory towers of philosophy and the sidewalks of our daily routines.

Selecting 100 philosophical ideas from thousands was not an easy task. However, I have tried to cover a wide range of ideas in this book. Even though this book is not meant to be an academic guide, you will have a good grasp of many complex philosophical concepts upon completion and will be able to understand most academic and serious philosophy books.

Writing this book has been an incredible journey for me. I am grateful to my family and friends who supported me throughout the process. I hope that this book helps people and reignites the love for philosophy among the common people.

Sincerely,

Daniel Chechick

Absolutism

"The more I see of the representatives of the people, the more I admire my dogs."

Alphonse de Lamartine

Absolutism is a philosophy that believes in giving all the power to one single ruler or authority figure, without sharing it with anyone else. This ruler has total control over the government, the laws, and the people.

Think of it like playing the game "Simon Says." In this game, there's a leader who gives commands, like "Simon says touch your nose." Everyone else has to follow those commands only if they start with "Simon says." The leader's word is absolute – there's no arguing or questioning their commands. They have all the power to make the rules and everyone else has to obey.

Now, let's apply this idea to rulers and governments. Imagine you live in a kingdom, and there's a king who is in charge of everything. The king doesn't have to follow any rules or listen to anyone else. He can make decisions without asking anyone's opinion. He has absolute power – just like in the game of "Simon Says."

Pros

Quick Decisions: With one ruler making all the decisions, things can happen faster. There's no need to wait for everyone to agree.

Stability: When one person is in control, there might be less arguing and fighting over what to do. This can bring stability to a country.

Cons

No Checks and Balances: Since there's no one to keep the ruler in check, they could make unfair or selfish choices without consequences.

History's Examples

Louis XIV of France: One famous historical example of absolutism is Louis XIV of France. He said, "I am the state," showing how much power he had. He made decisions without needing approval from anyone else.

Modern Perspective

Today, most countries don't have absolute rulers. They have governments with systems that share power among different branches and follow laws to protect people's rights. This helps avoid the problems that can come with one person having all the control.

So, Absolutism is like a game where the leader's commands are the only ones that matter. In history, some rulers had this kind of power, which had both advantages and disadvantages. Nowadays, most countries prefer a more balanced system of government to make sure everyone's voices are heard and to prevent any one person from having too much control.

Absurdism

"Reality is but a fleeting illusion, a dance of shadows orchestrated by the whims of perception."

Zephyr Kallias

Absurdism is a philosophy that suggests life doesn't have an inherent meaning, but people still search for meaning. This might sound a bit confusing, so let's break it down using a simple analogy.

It is like looking at life as if it's a super strange game that doesn't quite make sense. Imagine you're playing a video game, but the rules keep changing randomly, and the goals seem kind of weird. In this game, there's no ultimate purpose, and you're not sure why you're even playing. That's the essence of absurdism.

Think about it this way: you wake up each day and do all sorts of stuff, like going to school, hanging out with friends, and doing chores. These things might seem important, but when you zoom out, you realize that there's no big reason behind them. It's like trying to win a game that doesn't have a clear winner or a clear point.

Absurdism suggests that we humans are always searching for meaning in life, but we can never find a solid answer. It's as if we're playing a game that we didn't choose to play, and the rules are just made up as we go. This can sometimes make life feel confusing or even a bit funny because we're putting so much effort into things that might not have any real purpose.

Think about when you're trying to solve a tricky puzzle, and the pieces just don't fit together no matter how hard you try. You might start to wonder why you're even bothering with it. That's similar to how absurdism views life – as a puzzle that doesn't have a clear solution or a picture to complete.

Imagine going to a party where everyone is dancing to a song, but there's no music playing. You might join in because everyone else is doing it, but deep down, you know there's no actual reason for it. That's kind of how absurdism looks at our daily activities – we're doing things that seem important, but when we think about it, they might not be meaningful at all.

Absurdism encourages us to embrace this randomness and uncertainty. Instead of stressing out about finding a big meaning in life, we can focus on enjoying the small moments and finding joy in the absurdity itself. It's like laughing at the silliness of it all and creating your purpose in a world that doesn't have a set purpose.

So, absurdism is like playing a game where the rules are unclear, the goals are confusing, and the whole point might be a bit ridiculous. But instead of getting frustrated, we can have fun with the randomness and make our meaning along the way.

Agnosticism

"Have you ever noticed how 'What the hell' is always the right decision to make?"

Terry Johnson

Agnosticism is the belief that we cannot know for certain whether a higher power, like a god or gods, exists or not. It's like being unsure about whether aliens are living on distant planets. Some people believe in aliens, some don't, and some just say, "I don't know because I haven't seen enough evidence either way."

Imagine you're at a carnival, and there's a game where you have to guess how many jellybeans are in a jar. You might not be able to see inside the jar, and you don't have any information about how big the jar is or how many jelly beans were put in there. Agnosticism is a bit like saying, "I don't know how many jellybeans are in the jar because I don't have enough information to make a confident guess."

In daily life, agnosticism is when people admit that they don't have all the answers about things that can't be proven or seen. It's like when you wonder if ghosts are real or if there's life on other planets. Some people might believe in these things, some might not, and agnostics would say, "I can't say for sure because there's not enough evidence to prove or disprove it."

Agnosticism is not the same as atheism. Atheists don't believe in any gods, while agnostics don't claim to know for sure either way. It's as if you were trying to find out if a secret message was hidden in a book. An atheist might say, "I'm pretty sure there's no secret message in this book." An agnostic, on the other hand, would say, "I can't be certain if there's a secret message in the book because I haven't read the whole thing yet."

Being agnostic is about being open to possibilities and admitting that some things are just beyond our understanding. It's like looking at a big, mysterious box. You don't know what's inside, and you're not making any guesses until you have more information. Agnostics might say, "I don't know what's in the box, and I don't want to jump to conclusions without more evidence."

So, being agnostic means being honest about what you don't know and being open to learning more while respecting different viewpoints. It's like being at a crossroads and saying, "I'm not sure which path to take yet, but I'm willing to explore and discover."

Aestheticism

"Man is the only creature who refuses to be what he is."

Albert Camus

Aestheticism is a philosophy that emphasizes the beauty and enjoyment of art and nature for their own sake, rather than for any deeper meaning or practical purpose. It's about appreciating things just because they look or feel pleasing, without needing to find a hidden message or a practical use for them.

Think of it like enjoying a piece of cake. When you have a slice of cake, you don't necessarily need a reason beyond the fact that it tastes delicious and brings you joy. You're not trying to analyze the cake to find some profound meaning – you're simply savoring the flavors and enjoying the experience. Aestheticism is a bit like that but for art, nature, and other beautiful things.

Imagine you're walking in a garden full of colorful flowers. Aestheticism would be like stopping to admire those flowers, not because they have a specific purpose like providing food or medicine, but because they look stunning and make you feel happy. You're appreciating them purely for the visual pleasure they bring.

Likewise, when you listen to your favorite song, you're not always trying to decipher a deep message in the lyrics. You might be enjoying it just because the melody is catchy, and the rhythm is satisfying. Aestheticism encourages you to appreciate the song for the simple reason that it sounds beautiful to your ears.

In history, some artists embraced aestheticism by creating artworks that were meant to be enjoyed for their beauty alone. Imagine a painting of a serene landscape – you might not need to understand the historical context or the artist's personal story to find it breathtaking. The artwork's beauty is enough to captivate you.

Aestheticism doesn't mean ignoring the deeper meanings that art and nature can carry; it's more about allowing yourself to revel in beauty without feeling pressured to always dig for profound significance. It's like permitting yourself to enjoy a stunning sunset without needing to analyze why it feels so calming and wonderful.

So, whether you're gazing at a piece of art, reading a book, or simply enjoying the world around you, remember that aestheticism encourages you to appreciate things just because they're beautiful and bring joy to your senses. It's a reminder to let go of the need for everything to have a grand purpose and to relish the simple pleasure of experiencing beauty in its purest form.

Analytic Philosophy

"We have to dare to be ourselves, however frightening or strange that self may prove to be."

May Sarton

Analytic Philosophy is a branch of philosophy that focuses on breaking down complex ideas into smaller parts and using careful thinking to understand them better. It's like taking apart a complicated puzzle to figure out how each piece fits together.

Imagine you have a big jigsaw puzzle with thousands of pieces. Each piece represents an idea, a concept, or a question about the world. Analytic philosophers are like detectives who want to solve the puzzle of understanding these ideas. Instead of just looking at the whole picture, they zoom in on one piece at a time.

Let's say you have a puzzle piece that asks, "What is the meaning of 'truth'?" Instead of guessing an answer, an analytic philosopher would examine the piece closely. They might ask questions like, "What do we mean when we say something is 'true'?" or "How do we decide if a statement is true or false?" By carefully investigating these questions, they hope to put this puzzle piece in its right place.

One of the key tools analytic philosophers use is language. Just like detectives gather clues to solve a case, these philosophers use words and sentences to gather clues about the ideas they're studying. They're picky about how words are used because they want to make sure everyone understands each other clearly. It's like making sure everyone is speaking the same language during a global adventure.

Another thing that makes analytic philosophy special is its focus on logic. Think of logic as the rules that guide our thinking – it helps us make sense of things. Analytic philosophers use logic to make sure their arguments make sense and are based on good reasons. They're like architects building a strong and sturdy bridge of ideas, ensuring it won't collapse when challenged.

Let's go back to our puzzle analogy. Imagine you've figured out where a few pieces go, but there's still a big chunk missing. Analytic philosophers don't mind that there might be empty spots in the puzzle for a while. They're patient and careful, making sure each piece fits perfectly before moving on.

In summary, analytic philosophy is like solving a massive puzzle of ideas. It's about breaking down complex questions, using clear language, and applying logic to piece together our understanding of the world. So, if you enjoy exploring ideas like a detective and love solving puzzles, you might just be a future analytic philosopher!

Anarchism

"It is hard enough to remember my opinions, without also remembering my reasons for them!"

Friedrich Nietzsche

Anarchism is a philosophy that advocates for a society without centralized government or authority. In simple terms, it's the belief that people can live together in harmony and make decisions without a big boss telling them what to do.

Imagine you and your friends deciding where to go for a fun outing. Instead of one person being in charge and deciding everything, everyone gets to voice their ideas, and together you make a choice that everyone agrees on. Anarchism takes this idea and applies it to society as a whole.

Anarchists think that people can work together and make decisions without needing a government to tell them what's right or wrong. They believe in individual freedom and cooperation. It's like being part of a team where everyone respects each other's opinions and no one person has all the power.

However, just like in your group outing, problems might arise. Some people might want to go to the beach, while others prefer a park. Anarchists believe that in a society without a government, people can still find ways to solve disagreements. They might have community meetings or discussions to figure out the best solution for everyone.

An Important part of anarchism is equality. Anarchists think that no one should have more power or wealth than others. It's like playing a game where everyone starts with the same number of points. This way, everyone has a fair chance and nobody can boss others around.

Now, let's talk about rules. Anarchism doesn't mean chaos or no rules at all. It's more like having rules that everyone agrees on and follows because they make sense, not just because a government says so. Remember when you and your friends decided where to go? You probably agreed on things like not going somewhere too far or expensive. Anarchists think that rules should be made by the people they affect, just like you and your friends made rules for your outing.

Anarchism might sound dreamy, but it also faces challenges. Some people worry that without a strong government, things like roads, schools, and hospitals might not get built or maintained. Anarchists believe that people can come together to get things done, but these concerns are still debated.

In a way, anarchism is like being part of a big group project at school. Everyone has a say, and decisions are made together. The focus is on cooperation, fairness, and finding solutions that work for everyone. It's about believing in the power of people to work together without needing someone to boss them around.

ANTI-REALISM

"Never let your sense of morals prevent you from doing what is right."

Isaac Asimov

Anti-realism is a philosophical viewpoint that suggests that the things we perceive and believe in might not correspond directly to an objective reality outside of our thoughts. In simpler terms, it's the idea that what we think is real might not match up with what's out there.

Think of it like this: imagine you're watching a movie on a screen. The movie characters and the scenes they're in are like the things we experience in the world. Now, imagine that the screen is your mind, where you process and make sense of everything you see. Anti-realism is like saying that the movie you're watching on the screen might not exactly match up with the world outside the screen.

For example, consider the color blue. You might look at the sky and say it's blue. But is the blue you see the same for everyone? Some people might perceive it differently due to their eyes or how their brain processes colors. So, anti-realism suggests that the color blue you see might not be the same as the color blue someone else sees. It's like the movie screen (your mind) is showing slightly different versions of the same thing to different people.

Another way to understand anti-realism is by looking at language. We use words to describe things, like "tree" or "love." But what if the way you understand "love" is different from how someone else understands it? This idea shows that even our words might not perfectly capture the reality of what we're trying to describe.

In a more philosophical sense, anti-realism challenges the notion that there's one ultimate reality that everyone agrees on. Instead, it suggests that reality is shaped by our perceptions, thoughts, and experiences. Just like different people might have different opinions about a movie they watched, anti-realism proposes that our individual experiences can lead us to interpret and understand reality in slightly different ways.

So, anti-realism encourages us to be open-minded and consider that our views of reality might not be the same as others. It reminds us that what we think is real might just be a version of reality that our minds create based on our unique perspectives. Just like people might have different interpretations of a movie, anti-realism teaches us that our understanding of reality can be diverse and influenced by how we perceive the world.

Aristotelianism

"Do not fear to be eccentric in opinion, for every opinion now accepted was once eccentric."

Bertrand Russell

Aristotelianism is a philosophy that follows the ideas of Aristotle, an ancient Greek philosopher. This philosophy is all about looking at the world and understanding it through a logical and systematic approach.

For example, you're putting together a puzzle. Each puzzle piece represents a different part of the world – like animals, plants, people, and even ideas. Now, instead of randomly trying to fit the pieces together, you're using a guidebook that tells you how each piece connects to the others. This guidebook is like Aristotle's way of thinking.

Aristotle believed that everything in the world has a purpose, or what he called a "final cause." Just like a hammer is made for pounding nails, he thought that every living thing and even non-living things have a purpose that makes them unique. So, if you want to understand something, you need to figure out its purpose and how it works towards achieving that purpose.

Let's take another example: a tree. According to Aristotelianism, a tree's purpose is to grow, reproduce, and provide shade or resources. To understand a tree, you'd look at how it grows, what it needs to reproduce, and how it fits into the ecosystem.

But Aristotle didn't stop there. He also believed that the world is made up of different categories or "causes" that help explain why things are the way they are. These categories are like different angles to look at a situation. They include:

Material Cause: What something is made of. Like how a chair is made of wood.

Formal Cause: The shape or design that makes something what it is. For instance, the formal cause of a car is its structure and function as a vehicle.

Efficient Cause: The process or actions that lead to something coming into being. Think of this as the actions or efforts that bring a cake from a mix of ingredients to a baked dessert.

Final Cause: The purpose or goal that something is meant to achieve. We talked about this earlier with the puzzle pieces.

Aristotle's philosophy encourages people to observe, question, and think deeply about the world around them. Just like you're not satisfied with simply fitting puzzle pieces together – you want to understand how they fit and why they create a certain picture – Aristotelianism pushes you to explore the "whys" and "hows" of life.

Asceticism

"There may be times when we are powerless to prevent injustice, but there must never be a time when we fail to protest."

Elie Wiesel

Asceticism is a philosophy that involves self-discipline and a simple way of living to achieve spiritual or philosophical goals. It's like going to the gym for your mind and soul instead of your body.

Consider you're training for a marathon. You have to stick to a strict schedule of running, eating healthy, and resting properly. This disciplined routine helps you build endurance, strength, and mental focus. Asceticism is similar, but instead of training for a marathon, you're training your inner self.

In asceticism, people voluntarily choose to give up some of their comforts and desires. They might live with fewer material possessions, eat plain and simple food, and avoid luxury. Just like you would skip sugary snacks to stay in shape for your marathon, ascetics skip unnecessary indulgences to focus on their spiritual or philosophical journey.

Think of it as cleaning your room. You need to get rid of clutter, organize things neatly, and keep only what's essential. Ascetics do the same with their lives. By getting rid of unnecessary distractions, they create space for deeper thinking, self-reflection, and connection to their beliefs.

Imagine you're studying for an important exam. You set aside time to study every day, even when your friends are having fun. You might miss out on some immediate enjoyment, but you know that your hard work will pay off in the long run. Ascetics do something similar. They might avoid certain pleasures today because they believe it will lead to a more fulfilling and meaningful life in the future.

Just as an athlete needs to resist the temptation to skip training or cheat on their diet, ascetics need to resist the pull of materialistic desires or instant gratification. It's not about punishing yourself, but about building inner strength and resilience.

In summary, asceticism is like training for your mind and soul. Just as athletes sacrifice short-term indulgences for long-term success, ascetics give up unnecessary comforts to achieve deeper spiritual or philosophical growth. It's about simplifying your life, building inner strength, and focusing on what truly matters to you.

ATHEOLOGICAL

"I was within and without, simultaneously enchanted and repelled by the inexhaustible variety of life."

Fitzgerald F. Scott

Atheological is a philosophical term that explores the concept of the absence or non-existence of God. It delves into discussions and inquiries about the nature of the divine, questioning whether there is a higher power or if the universe operates without the guidance of a supreme being.

Analogical Insight: Imagine you are playing a video game. In this game, there are characters, a storyline, and a vast virtual world. Now, consider the idea that there might not be a game designer behind it all, no one orchestrating the plot or controlling the characters. Atheological thinking is a bit like questioning whether there's a game designer, or if the game simply exists on its own, running its course without someone intentionally steering its direction.

Now, let's unpack this concept a bit more.

Exploring the Absence of God: Atheological thinking doesn't outright deny the existence of God but rather examines the world without assuming a divine presence. It's like reading a book without assuming there's an author. Atheology invites us to consider the possibility that the universe and everything in it might operate according to natural laws and principles, without the need for a creator pulling the strings.

The Universe as a Self-Running System: Think of the universe as a self-running machine. Everything happens according to a set of rules, like the laws of physics. Planets orbit, seasons change, and living things grow and evolve, all following a predetermined order. Atheological philosophy asks whether this intricate system could exist without a conscious creator behind it, much like a clock ticking away without someone winding it up.

Seeking Answers through Reason and Evidence: Atheology relies on reason and evidence rather than accepting beliefs based solely on faith. Picture a detective solving a mystery. Instead of relying on gut feelings or ancient scrolls, the detective examines clues, gathers evidence, and uses logical thinking to unravel the truth. Similarly, atheological thinkers rely on scientific discoveries, observations, and critical thinking to understand the world around them.

Morality Without Divine Guidance: Atheological pondering extends to questions of morality. Traditionally, many believe that morality comes from religious teachings, but atheological thinking asks whether humans can be good and ethical without a divine rulebook. It's like considering if people can play fair in the game of life without an external referee.

The Diversity of Atheological Perspectives: Atheology isn't a one-size-fits-all philosophy. Just as people have different opinions about the best way to play a game, atheological thinkers may have diverse perspectives. Some may argue that the absence of evidence for God leads them to atheological conclusions, while others might emphasize the importance of critical thinking and personal experience.

Conclusion: In the grand scheme of philosophical exploration, atheology is like putting on a pair of glasses that allows us to see the world without assuming a divine presence. It's a lens through which we question, ponder, and seek understanding based on reason and evidence. Like exploring the vast landscapes of a video game, atheological thinking invites us to navigate the complexities of life with curiosity and an open mind, considering the possibility that the universe is its masterful creation.

AUTHENTICITY

"We are all atheists about most of the gods that humanity has ever believed in. Some of us just go one god further."

Richard Dawkins

Authenticity is a philosophical term that means being true to yourself and your values. It's like staying real and honest with who you are, no matter what.

Imagine you're a unique puzzle piece. Being authentic is about fitting into the puzzle of life in a way that feels right for you. It's not about pretending to be someone else or following what others do. It's about embracing your quirks, passions, and beliefs, and letting them shine.

Think about your favorite song. When the singer pours their heart into the lyrics, you can feel their authenticity. It's the same in life. When you're authentic, you're like that favorite song – genuine, unfiltered, and full of emotion.

Authenticity is like having a secret ingredient that makes you stand out. Just like a cake with a surprise filling, being true to yourself adds a special flavor to the world. It's tempting to blend in, but authenticity encourages you to be bold and let your true colors show.

Sometimes, it might seem easier to wear a mask and act like someone you're not. But that's like painting over a beautiful canvas with someone else's colors. Authenticity is about owning your canvas, even if it's not like everyone else's. Your canvas tells a story, and that story matters.

Remember the feeling of chatting with your best friend? You can be totally yourself – goofy jokes, dreams, and all. Authenticity is like being your own best friend. It's treating yourself with the same kindness and acceptance that you give to your closest pals.

In a world where trends and opinions change like the weather, authenticity is your constant. It's like your anchor, grounding you in your beliefs and values. When you stay true to yourself, you build a strong foundation that can weather any storm.

So, authenticity is like a precious gem you carry within you. It's about embracing your uniqueness, being honest with yourself, and letting your true self shine. Remember, you're the author of your story, and authenticity is what makes each chapter meaningful and real.

Autonomism

"You're not to be so blind with patriotism that you can't face reality. Wrong is wrong, no matter who does it or says it."

Malcolm X

Autonomism is a philosophy that believes in the importance of self-governing and making your own decisions. In other words, it's about valuing your independence and having control over your own choices and actions.

Think of it like driving a car. Imagine you're learning to drive for the first time. In the beginning, you might have a driving instructor next to you, telling you when to turn, when to stop, and how to park. They're like an authority figure guiding you. But as you practice more and gain experience, you start to feel more confident. You begin making decisions on your own – when to change lanes, when to slow down, and when to take a turn.

Just like in driving, there are times when you might encounter roadblocks or unexpected situations. With autonomism, you're encouraged to come up with creative solutions and adapt to these challenges. Instead of always waiting for someone else to tell you what to do, you learn to trust your own instincts and problem-solving skills.

Autonomism is also connected to the idea of individuality. It recognizes that each person has their own unique experiences, feelings, and perspectives. Just as no two people drive in the same way, nobody lives their life exactly like someone else. Autonomism encourages you to embrace your individuality and make choices that align with your values and goals.

Of course, becoming autonomous doesn't happen overnight. It's a gradual process that involves learning, reflecting, and growing. Just like how you become a better driver with practice, you become more autonomous by making decisions, learning from your experiences, and becoming more self-aware.

BEHAVIORISM

"We have to dare to be ourselves, however frightening or strange that self may prove to be."

May Sarton

Behaviorism is a philosophy that suggests we can understand and predict human behavior by focusing solely on observable actions and reactions while ignoring thoughts, emotions, and mental processes. It's like studying a video game character's moves without worrying about what they're thinking or feeling.

Consider you're playing a video game where you control a character. The game records every move your character makes – jumping, running, shooting, and more. Now, let's say you want to understand and predict how your character will act in different situations. You decide to use a philosophy called behaviorism.

Behaviorism is like looking at the game screen and only paying attention to what your character does. You don't care about what your character might be thinking or feeling. You don't wonder if your character is scared of an enemy or excited to find a treasure. Instead, you focus on the actions your character takes in response to the game's challenges.

In the same way, behaviorism in real life focuses only on what people do, not what's happening in their minds. Behaviorists believe that if we watch and measure how someone behaves in different situations, we can understand and even predict their future actions, just like you can predict your video game character's moves based on their past actions.

However, it's important to know that not everyone agrees with behaviorism. Some people think that understanding behavior requires looking at both actions and what's happening inside someone's mind. They believe that thoughts, feelings, and experiences are important pieces of the puzzle too.

So, next time you're playing a video game, remember that just like behaviorism helps you understand your character's actions, it's a philosophy that helps us understand human behavior by looking only at what people do, without thinking about what's going on inside their minds.

BIOETHICS

"The reasonable man adapts himself to the world: the unreasonable one persists in trying to adapt the world to himself. Therefore all progress depends on the unreasonable man."

George Bernard Shaw

Bioethics is a field of philosophy that deals with the ethical questions and dilemmas that arise from advances in biology, medicine, and healthcare. It's like being the referee in a game, making sure that everyone plays fairly and follows the rules.

Imagine you're playing a video game with your friends. There are certain rules that everyone agrees to follow to make the game fun and fair. Now, think of life as a big game where doctors, scientists, and researchers are the players. They make discoveries and create amazing things, just like players find new strategies and unlock new levels in a game.

But here's the catch: in the game of life, the rules aren't always clear, and the decisions people make can have a big impact on others. This is where bioethics comes in. It's like having a rulebook that helps everyone understand what's right and wrong when it comes to medicine, science, and how we treat living things.

Bioethics looks at tough questions. For example, imagine a doctor has a new technology that can help people walk again, but it's very expensive. Should only rich people have access to it, or should everyone get a chance? That's a fairness question – just like in a game, where you want to make sure everyone has an equal chance to win.

Bioethics also deals with questions about life and death. Imagine a person is sick and can't get better. Is it okay to stop trying to help them? This is a difficult decision, like choosing whether to continue playing a game that's not fun anymore. Bioethics helps people decide when it's time to stop and let go.

Remember how in games, players sometimes cheat? Well, in the real world, people might want to do things that aren't quite fair or that might hurt others. Bioethics helps us set boundaries and decide what's acceptable. It's like making sure everyone follows the rules so that the game of life stays fair and everyone has a chance to win.

In a nutshell, bioethics is like the referee of the game of life. It helps us make fair decisions about medicine, science, and how we treat living things. Just as a referee ensures that everyone follows the rules and plays fairly, bioethics guides us in making ethical choices and finding the right path in the world of biology and healthcare.

Cameralism

"I cannot teach anybody anything. I can only make them think."

Socrates

Cameralism is a philosophy that emerged in Europe during the 17th and 18th centuries. It's not about cameras or photography, but rather a way of thinking about how a state or government should be organized and run. Let's break it down in a way that's easy to understand.

Imagine your family home. In your home, there are certain rules and responsibilities to make sure everything runs smoothly. Your parents might budget the money, plan meals, and make sure everyone is safe and healthy. This is kind of like what cameralism suggests for a government but on a much larger scale.

In a government based on cameralism, the rulers act like parents, and the citizens are like the children of a big family. The government's main job is to take care of its citizens, just like your parents take care of you. Here's how cameralism works:

Economic Management: Just like your parents budget money for things like food, clothes, and bills, a government practicing cameralism would manage the country's money carefully. They would make sure there's enough money to build schools, hospitals, and infrastructure, and also to keep the country safe.

Education: In your family, your parents might make sure you and your siblings go to school to learn and become responsible adults. Similarly, a cameralist government would provide education for all citizens to help them grow and contribute to society.

Health and Safety: Just as your parents want to keep you safe and healthy, a cameralist government would work to ensure the safety and well-being of its citizens. This means having police to maintain order and hospitals to care for the sick.

Public Works: Think of your home with electricity, clean water, and good roads. A cameralist government would provide these things to everyone in the country to improve their quality of life.

Social Welfare: Just as your parents may provide support and care when you need it, a cameralist government might have programs to help people who are struggling, like the elderly, disabled, or unemployed.

Order and Discipline: In a well-managed household, there are rules to keep things in order. Similarly, a cameralist government would have laws and rules to ensure that everyone is treated fairly and that there is peace and order in society.

Keep in mind that while cameralism had its time in history, different philosophies and ideas about government have evolved over the years. Each philosophy has its strengths and weaknesses, and governments today often use a mix of ideas to create a system that works for their country.

So, cameralism is an interesting part of the history of political thought, but it's not the only way to organize a government.

CASUISTRY

"A truth that's told with bad intent beats all the lies you can invent."

William Blake

Casuistry is a philosophical term that means making moral decisions by looking at specific cases or situations rather than relying on strict rules. It's like being a detective who solves each case based on the unique evidence you find, rather than following a set list of rules for every situation.

In casuistry, you wouldn't just follow one rule for every case. Instead, you'd carefully examine the details of each crime individually and make decisions based on the specific circumstances.

Let's break this down a bit more:

No One-Size-Fits-All Rules: Casuistry says that moral decisions can't always be made by applying the same rule to every situation. So, just like a detective doesn't solve every case with the same approach, you don't judge every moral dilemma with the same rule.

Looking at the Details: Just like a detective collects evidence, casuistry focuses on gathering all the facts and details about a specific situation. For example, if you're deciding whether it's okay to borrow a friend's phone, you'd consider factors like whether your friend is comfortable with it, if they need their phone at that moment, or if it's an emergency.

Balancing Act: Casuistry involves a bit of a balancing act. You weigh the pros and cons, just like a detective weighs the evidence for and against a suspect. You'd think about the potential benefits of borrowing the phone (maybe you need to call for help) against the potential drawbacks (your friend might be in the middle of something important).

Flexibility: Casuistry allows for flexibility. It's like a detective adapting to different crime scenes. Sometimes, the same rule might apply, but often, you'll need to consider the details to make the right choice.

Casuistry is like having a toolkit of moral thinking. It's about being thoughtful, considering the specifics of each situation, and making the best ethical choice based on what you know. Remember, life isn't always black and white, and casuistry helps you find the right shade of grey when you're making moral decisions.

Cognitive relativism

"Those who know do not speak. Those who speak do not know."

Lao Tsu

Cognitive Relativism is a philosophical term that means different people can have their truths and beliefs, and these can all be valid in their way. It's like saying there can be many paths to the same destination.

Imagine you and your friend are standing on opposite sides of a very big mountain. You both want to describe what you see. Your friend says, "I see trees and a river," while you say, "I see rocks and a lake." Both descriptions are true, but they're also different. It's because you're looking at the mountain from different angles.

In the same way, cognitive relativism says that people's ideas and beliefs can be true for them, just like the descriptions of the mountain. What you believe can be different from what your friend believes, and both can be right in their way.

Cognitive relativism is about respecting other people's thoughts and beliefs, even if they're not the same as yours. It's like understanding that different paths can lead to the same goal. So, when you meet someone with different ideas, instead of saying they're wrong, you can say, "That's your perspective, and it's valid for you."

However, there's a balance to keep in mind. While cognitive relativism encourages us to respect different beliefs, it doesn't mean that everything is equally valid. For example, if someone believes that jumping off a cliff without a parachute will be safe, that's not a valid belief because it goes against what we know about gravity and safety. It's important to remember that some things are based on facts and evidence, and those should be trusted over beliefs that don't match reality.

Constructivism

"Science is not only compatible with spirituality; it is a profound source of spirituality."

Carl Sagan

Constructivism, in philosophy, is the idea that our understanding of the world is not just a passive reflection of how things are, but it's actively built or "constructed" by our minds.

Imagine you're building a treehouse. You start with some wooden planks, nails, and a vision of what you want it to look like. As you begin building, you make choices – where to put each plank, how to angle the roof, and what color to paint it. These choices shape your treehouse, and it becomes a unique creation that reflects your ideas and preferences.

Similarly, constructivism suggests that our understanding of the world is like building that treehouse. We don't just passively absorb information like sponges. Instead, we actively interact with the world, shaping our understanding based on our experiences, thoughts, and choices.

When you see something, like a tree, your brain doesn't just take a photograph of it. It interprets the information it receives through your senses. It decides what's important, what to ignore, and how to make sense of it. This interpretation is influenced by your past experiences, cultural background, and personal beliefs.

Constructivism is all about understanding that your mind is an active builder of knowledge. You construct your understanding of the world through a combination of perception, learning, thoughts, social interactions, and cultural influences. Just like your treehouse is unique to you, your understanding of the world is unique to you as well. It's always evolving and changing as you gather more tools and have new experiences.

Continental philosophy

"A paranoid is someone who knows a little of what's going on."

William S. Burroughs

Continental philosophy is a branch of philosophy that's a bit like exploring a rich and diverse jungle of ideas. It's all about digging deep into the complex and often messy aspects of human existence.

Think of philosophy like a big tree with different branches. One of those branches is called "analytic philosophy." It's like a tree that's been carefully pruned and shaped, with each branch neatly organized. Analytic philosophers like to trim away anything that isn't precise or clear, so they can focus on specific questions with straightforward answers. It's like trying to solve a puzzle with well-defined pieces.

Now, imagine another tree, wild and untamed, with branches growing in all directions. That's where continental philosophy comes in. It's a bit like exploring the jungle around this tree. Continental philosophers are more interested in the messy, complicated parts of life. They ask questions like, "What does it mean to be human?" or "How do we make sense of our existence?" These questions don't always have clear-cut answers; they're more like trying to find your way through a dense forest filled with twists and turns.

One big difference is in the style of writing. Analytic philosophers tend to write in a very precise and structured way, like a well-organized textbook. Continental philosophers, on the other hand, often write in a more poetic and exploratory style. They might use stories, metaphors, and even personal experiences to help us understand the deep, murky parts of life.

Continental philosophy is like a toolbox filled with different tools for exploring the jungle of human existence. Some philosophers in this tradition, like Jean-Paul Sartre, might use the machete of existentialism to cut through the underbrush of meaninglessness. Others, like Simone de Beauvoir, might use the compass of feminism to navigate the terrain of gender and identity. Each tool helps us explore a different aspect of this complex jungle.

CRITICAL REALISM

"Grown-ups never understand anything by themselves, and it is tiresome for children to be always and forever explaining things to them."

Antoine de Saint-Exupéry

Critical realism is a philosophy that helps us understand the world around us, especially when it comes to science and how we know things. Let me break it down for you in a simple way.

Critical realism is like looking at a painting. It suggests that what we see in the painting might not be exactly what's in the real world, but it's the closest we can get to understanding it.

Critical realism says that the painting is like our knowledge of the world. It's a representation, like a map, but it's not the real thing. In the real forest, there might be things the painting can't show, like the sounds, smells, or even what's happening behind the trees. The painting can't capture everything.

Here are three key ideas of critical realism:

The Real World Exists:- Critical realism says there is a real world out there, even if we can't see or understand everything about it. Just like there's a real forest even if the painting can't show it all.

Our Knowledge is Limited:- It recognizes that our understanding of the world is limited. We can't know everything, and sometimes, our ideas might be wrong, just like the painting can't show every detail of the forest.

We Can Get Closer to the Truth:- Even though our knowledge is limited, we can keep improving it. Just like artists can get better at painting, scientists and thinkers can get closer and closer to understanding the real world by studying it and thinking critically.

Critical realism is a bit like a reminder to stay humble about what we know. It tells us that we should keep trying to learn more and get closer to the truth, even if we know we might never see the whole picture.

Cultural determinism

"If a cluttered desk is a sign of a cluttered mind, of what, then, is an empty desk a sign?"

Laurence J. Peter

Cultural determinism is a philosophical idea that suggests our culture, the environment we grow up in, and the society we live in, play a significant role in shaping who we are and how we think. It proposes that these factors largely determine our beliefs, values, behaviors, and even our potential in life. Think of it as a bit like a recipe that influences the way we turn out as individuals.

Each ingredient you put into the soup represents a different aspect of your culture and environment. These ingredients include your family, the place you were born, the language you speak, the traditions you follow, and the people you surround yourself with. Just like the ingredients in a soup give it a particular taste, your cultural ingredients give you a unique identity and worldview.

Your family is like the base of the soup. They provide you with your first taste of culture. The values, beliefs, and habits your family has are often passed down to you. For example, if your family values honesty and hard work, you're likely to adopt those values too. Language is a key ingredient. It not only helps you communicate but also carries with it a whole set of cultural meanings. The language you speak can influence how you express yourself and even how you think. Traditions are like spices in your cultural soup. They add unique flavors and customs to your life. For instance, celebrating certain holidays or participating in specific ceremonies can be a big part of your cultural identity. Your friends and the people you spend time with can also flavor your cultural soup. If you hang out with friends who love music, you might develop a passion for it too. If they have certain beliefs or interests, you might find yourself sharing those as well.

However, here's the interesting part: While cultural determinism says these ingredients have a strong impact, it doesn't mean you have no say in the final flavor of your soup. You can add your seasonings as you grow and learn. You can explore new ingredients by meeting people from different cultures, learning new languages, or traveling to new places.

Cultural Relativism

"There is nothing either good or bad, but thinking makes it so."

William Shakespeare

Cultural Relativism is a philosophy that suggests that the beliefs, values, and practices of a particular culture should be understood and judged in the context of that culture itself, rather than being compared to the beliefs, values, or practices of another culture. In simpler terms, it's like realizing that different places have different rules for games, and those rules are okay as long as everyone playing understands and agrees with them.

Let's call it "Game X." In Game X, there are certain rules you all follow. These rules might include how to score points, what's considered fair play, and how you determine the winner. You and your friends are having a great time playing Game X, and you all agree on these rules because they make the game fun and fair.

Now, imagine that in a different part of the world, there's another group of friends playing a similar game called "Game Y." However, the rules for Game Y are quite different from those of Game X. They have their way of scoring points, their ideas about what's fair, and their way of deciding the winner. Just like you and your friends, they enjoy playing Game Y because it makes sense to them and adds excitement to their playtime.

Cultural Relativism is like looking at both Game X and Game Y and saying, "Each of these games is great in its way because the rules work for the people playing them." It means you don't judge Game Y by the rules of Game X or vice versa. You respect that different groups have different ways of doing things, and that's perfectly fine as long as everyone involved is happy with the rules.

There are some important things to remember about Cultural Relativism. It doesn't mean we have to agree with everything in every culture. If a cultural practice harms people or goes against basic human rights, it's still important to speak up against it. For example, if a culture were to condone harming others for fun, most people would agree that this is wrong, no matter what that culture believes. So, Cultural Relativism doesn't mean we should blindly accept everything; it just means we should try to understand and respect cultural differences whenever we can.

Cynicism

"The Cynic knows only his own worth; the world estimates him according to his success."

Johann Kaspar Lavater

Cynicism, in philosophy, is a belief that people are often motivated by self-interest, and they may not always act honestly or with good intentions. It's like when you suspect someone might have hidden motives behind their actions, rather than just doing something because it's the right thing to do.

Let's call them Alex. Alex is always offering to help you with your homework, but you can't help but wonder why. Is it because they genuinely want to help you succeed, or do they have a hidden agenda? Maybe they want something from you in return, like answers to the upcoming math test.

In the world of cynicism, you might lean towards thinking that Alex isn't being completely altruistic. You might believe that they're helping you because they see a benefit for themselves, not just because they're kind-hearted. This suspicion is at the core of cynicism.

Cynics are like professional detectives of human behavior. They look beyond the surface and question people's motives. They often believe that most actions, even seemingly good ones, are driven by self-interest. It's not that cynics don't believe in acts of kindness; it's more about being cautious and skeptical about people's true intentions.

Now, cynicism isn't always a bad thing. It can help you be aware of potential ulterior motives and protect yourself from being taken advantage of. But on the flip side, it can make you a bit skeptical and less trusting of others. Imagine if you were always suspicious of your friends and family, never taking their actions at face value. That could strain your relationships.

Think of cynicism as a pair of glasses. When you put them on, you see the world through a different lens—one that's more critical and suspicious. But sometimes, you need to take those glasses off to appreciate the genuine kindness and good intentions that exist in the world.

It encourages us to question, but not to always assume the worst. So, as you navigate life, remember that while cynicism can be a useful tool, it's essential to strike a balance between being cautious and giving people the benefit of the doubt. After all, not everything is as it seems, but not everything is as cynical as it might appear either.

Daoism

"By letting it go, it all gets done. The world is won by those who let it go. But when you try and try, the world is beyond the winning."

Laozi

Daoism, also spelled Taoism, is a philosophical way of thinking that originated in ancient China. At its core, Daoism revolves around the idea of "Dao" (pronounced "dow"), which is a fundamental concept in this philosophy.

Imagine Dao as a river. This river represents the natural flow of life, the way things are meant to be. Daoism teaches us to go with the flow of this river, to embrace the natural order of things rather than fighting against it.

In Daoism, there's a belief that when we resist the natural course of events when we try to force things to happen the way we want them to, we often create problems and suffering for ourselves. It's like trying to swim upstream against a powerful current. It's exhausting, and you might not get very far.

On the other hand, when we learn to flow with the Dao, like floating downstream with the current, life becomes easier and more harmonious. It's about finding the path of least resistance and making the most of what life offers without trying to control everything.

Daoism also emphasizes the importance of simplicity and living in harmony with nature. Think of how a tree grows, or how a river flows effortlessly. Daoists believe that by simplifying our lives and aligning ourselves with the natural world, we can find peace and balance.

Another essential concept in Daoism is "Yin" and "Yang." These are like the balance of opposites. Yin is the dark, passive, and receptive side, while Yang is the bright, active, and assertive side. Daoism teaches that these opposites are interconnected and interdependent, and true harmony comes from balancing them in our lives, just like the balance between day and night.

Meditation and mindfulness are also practices embraced by Daoists. By quieting the mind and being present now, we can better connect with the Dao and understand its subtle influence on our lives. It's like standing by the river and simply listening to the sound of flowing water, without trying to change it.

In Daoism, there's a deep respect for the individual's unique path. It encourages us to discover our way of living in harmony with the Dao, recognizing that everyone's river is a little different. It's about being true to yourself and not trying to imitate others. Just as a tree bends with the wind and a river follows its course, Daoism teaches us to go with the flow of life and find our unique path within it.

DECONSTRUCTIONISM

"Life is really simple, but we insist on making it complicated."

Confucius

Deconstructionism is a philosophical term that might sound complex, but we can break it down into simpler ideas. At its core, deconstructionism is like taking apart a puzzle to see how it was made, but with words and ideas instead of puzzle pieces.

Imagine you have a story, like a fairy tale. Deconstructionism is like examining that story closely, not just to enjoy the tale but to see how it's put together. It's like looking at the individual words, sentences, and ideas that make up the story.

Here's a more formal definition: Deconstructionism is a way of thinking about texts, like books, essays, or even movies, that tries to uncover hidden meanings and contradictions by closely analyzing the words and ideas within them. It was developed by a philosopher named Jacques Derrida.

Now, let's dive deeper into how deconstructionism works with our fairy tale example:

Words and Meanings: Deconstructionism looks at the words used in the story and how they might have different meanings. For example, the word "freedom" might mean different things to different people. Deconstructionists ask, "What does 'freedom' really mean in this story? How do the characters understand it?"

Contradictions: It also looks for contradictions or conflicting ideas within the story. Imagine if our fairy tale said, "The princess lived happily ever after, but she was always sad." Deconstructionists would ask, "How can she be happy and sad at the same time? What does this contradiction tell us about the story's message?"

Hidden Messages: Deconstructionism believes that there are often hidden messages or biases in stories. It's like reading between the lines. In our fairy tale, if the hero is always a prince and never a princess, deconstructionists might wonder why that is. What does it say about the roles of men and women in this story?

Unanswered Questions: Sometimes, deconstructionism focuses on what the story doesn't tell us. It's like noticing what's missing in the puzzle. If our fairy tale never explains why the evil witch is so wicked, deconstructionists might ask, "What's the backstory here? Why is she the way she is?"

Different Perspectives: Deconstructionism also considers that different people might interpret the same story in various ways. It's like seeing the same painting but having different feelings about it. So, it asks, "How might different readers see this fairy tale differently? What personal experiences shape their views?"

It wants to uncover all the layers of meaning, even the ones that aren't obvious. It's about questioning, analyzing, and thinking deeply about the words and ideas that make up the stories we read and hear.

It reminds us that there's often more to a story than meets the eye and that understanding these hidden layers can give us a richer and more thoughtful appreciation of literature and ideas.

DEEP ECOLOGY

"I don't know what's worse: to not know what you are and be happy, or to become what you've always wanted to be, and feel alone."

Daniel Keyes

Deep Ecology is a philosophy that sees nature as more than just a resource for humans to use. It suggests that all living things have an intrinsic value, meaning they're valuable in and of themselves, not just because they're useful to us. To understand this better, think of it like a big, intricate web.

Picture a spider's web in a garden. Each strand of silk connects to another, forming a complex structure. Now, imagine that every thread represents a living thing on Earth – plants, animals, and even humans. Deep Ecology says that each thread, no matter how small or seemingly insignificant, has value.

In traditional ways of thinking, we often view nature as something separate from us, like a tool to meet our needs. It's like thinking of the web as just a bunch of individual threads. We might only pay attention to the threads that directly benefit us, like the ones we can use to swing from branch to branch. The rest of the threads, the ones we don't use, seem less important.

Deep Ecology challenges this view. It asks us to see the web as a whole, where every thread matters. Even the threads we don't use are crucial to the web's stability. If we remove too many threads, the web weakens, and the whole structure can collapse. In the same way, if we harm the environment or destroy species without thinking about their value beyond what they can do for us, we risk damaging the delicate balance of nature.

Determinism

"A serious and good philosophical work could be written consisting entirely of jokes."

Ludwig Wittgenstein

Determinism is a philosophical concept that suggests that every event, including our actions and choices, is the result of prior events and circumstances, and is therefore predictable if we know all the factors involved. In simpler terms, it's the idea that everything that happens in the world is like a line of dominoes falling one after another, each domino causing the next to fall in a specific, pre-determined way.

Each domino represents an event or a moment in time. Now, let's say we set up these dominoes in such a way that if we push the first one, it will knock down the second one, which will knock down the third one, and so on. If we know the size and spacing of the dominoes, the force we apply to the first one, and the condition of the table, we can predict exactly how all the dominoes will fall.

In the same way, determinism suggests that if we knew everything about the universe at a particular moment – the position and speed of every particle, the state of every atom, and all the laws of nature – we could predict with absolute certainty everything that will happen next. This includes not only natural events like the movement of planets but also human actions and decisions.

Now, let's think about how this applies to our lives. Imagine you're trying to decide what to have for breakfast. Determinism says that your choice isn't free. It's the result of a long chain of causes and effects. Maybe your choice is influenced by what food is available in your kitchen, what you ate yesterday, your hunger level, your personal preferences, and even the advertisements you've seen recently. All these factors combine to determine what you'll choose for breakfast, and you might not even realize it.

Some people find this idea unsettling because it seems to suggest that we don't have true freedom or control over our lives. It's as if we're just puppets following a script that was written long ago by the conditions of the universe.

There are different interpretations of determinism. Some philosophers believe in "soft determinism," which suggests that while our actions are influenced by prior events, we can still make meaningful choices within those influences. Others argue for "hard determinism," which posits that our choices are entirely preordained.

So, while determinism raises thought-provoking questions about the nature of free will and the predictability of our actions, it's a complex and debated topic in philosophy. It challenges us to think deeply about the relationship between cause and effect, the boundaries of our choices, and the true extent of our control over our lives. Ultimately, whether we are truly free or bound by determinism is a question that continues to intrigue and inspire philosophers and thinkers of all ages.

Digital Philosophy

"Be kind, for everyone you meet is fighting a hard battle."

Socrates

Digital Philosophy is a branch of philosophy that explores the fundamental nature of reality in the context of digital information and computation. To put it simply, it's like asking whether the entire universe can be thought of as one massive computer program.

Imagine you're playing a video game, like Minecraft. In the game, everything you see and interact with – the trees, the animals, the buildings – is made up of tiny blocks. These blocks are like the basic units of the game's world. You can build, destroy, and manipulate these blocks to create your virtual reality.

Now, let's apply this idea to the real world. Digital Philosophy suggests that just like those blocks in Minecraft, everything in the universe, including you and me, might be made up of tiny "digital" units. These units, in our case, could be something like atoms or even smaller particles.

Think of these tiny units as the building blocks of reality. They can combine and interact in various ways, just like the blocks in the game. Everything we see, touch, and experience in the world could be a result of these digital-like units coming together and following certain rules, just like how the game's blocks follow rules to create the game world.

Now, you might be wondering, why would anyone believe this? Well, there are a few reasons. One is that when scientists study the very, very small building blocks of our universe, like atoms and subatomic particles, they sometimes find behaviors that resemble the way information is processed in computers. This similarity has led some thinkers to suggest that the universe operates like a giant, incredibly complex computer.

Another reason is the idea of simulation. Have you ever played a simulation game, like The Sims? In these games, you create and control characters and watch them interact in a simulated world. Digital Philosophy asks, what if our universe is like a simulation created by some incredibly advanced beings or forces? In this view, everything we experience is part of this grand simulation, and what we perceive as reality is just the output of this cosmic computer program.

In the end, whether you're a believer in Digital Philosophy or not, it's a concept that encourages us to question the nature of our reality and the way we perceive the world. It's like looking at the universe through the lens of a computer screen, wondering if the code of existence is written in the language of bits and bytes.

Ecological Rationality

"Man suffers only because he takes seriously what the gods made for fun."

Alan Wilson Watts

Ecological Rationality is a way of making decisions that are based on what works best in the real world, rather than following strict rules or overthinking things.

Suppose you're playing a game, like soccer. You don't have a rulebook in your head telling you exactly what to do in every situation, right? You don't stop and think, "Okay, the rulebook says I should kick the ball with my right foot now." No, that would be too slow and not very effective.

Instead, you use your instincts and experience. You see the field, you see your teammates, and you decide at the moment what's the best move. Maybe you pass the ball, maybe you dribble, or maybe you take a shot. You make these decisions based on what feels right in that situation.

That's where ecological rationality comes in. It's like playing soccer. It's about using your brain in a way that makes sense for the situation you're in.

Here's another example: Imagine you're in the forest, and you see a bear. You don't need a book to tell you what to do, right? You don't think, "Hmm, the rulebook says I should slowly back away." No! You run! Your brain tells you to run because it knows that's the best thing to do when you see a bear.

So, ecological rationality is about using your brain like that. It's about being smart in the real world, not just following rules blindly. It's like playing soccer or running from a bear – you use your instincts and what you know to make the best decision for the situation.

Now, why is this important? Well, the world is full of situations that are way too complex to have strict rules for. Life doesn't come with a rulebook. Think about making new friends, choosing a career, or solving problems – there's no one-size-fits-all answer. Ecological rationality helps you navigate these situations by trusting your judgment and adapting to what's happening around you.

Emergentism

"The first duty of a man is to think for himself."

Jose Marti

Emergentism is a philosophical idea that suggests complex things can "emerge" from simpler parts. For example, consider a human brain. It's made up of billions of tiny cells called neurons. These neurons are like our LEGO blocks. On their own, they're not very smart, just like individual LEGO pieces aren't very exciting. But when you put billions of neurons together and they start talking to each other, you get something amazing: consciousness, thoughts, and emotions. Emergentism tells us that our mind emerges from the combined activity of these simple neurons, just like a big castle emerges from lots of tiny LEGO blocks.

Another way to think about it is through water. Imagine you have a pot of water, and you start heating it. As the temperature rises, something interesting happens: the water goes from being calm to boiling. This sudden change is an emergence. The heat from the tiny water molecules bouncing around creates this big change in the state of the water – from liquid to gas. Emergentism tells us that sometimes when you put simple things together and they interact in just the right way, you can get unexpected and complex results.

So, whether we're talking about the brain, a bustling city, or even the behavior of a crowd at a concert, emergentism helps us understand how simple parts can come together to create something much greater than the sum of its pieces.

Epistemic Humility

"The first principle is that you must not fool yourself — and you are the easiest person to fool." -

Richard P. Feynman

Epistemic humility is a philosophical term that might sound complex, but it's all about staying open-minded and recognizing that we don't know everything. Let's break it down into simpler terms.

Epistemic humility is the idea that we should approach knowledge and beliefs with a sense of modesty and openness. It means admitting that we might be wrong or that there's always more to learn.

Think of it like this: Imagine you're on a treasure hunt, searching for a hidden treasure chest. You have a map, but it's not a perfect map. It might have some mistakes, or maybe it's incomplete. Epistemic humility is like recognizing that your map might not be 100% accurate.

Let's dive deeper into what this concept means:

Admitting Our Map Could Be Wrong: In our treasure hunt analogy, this means acknowledging that the map might lead us astray. In real life, it's about accepting that our beliefs and knowledge might have errors. Instead of being overly confident, we should be open to the possibility that we're mistaken.

Being Open to New Clues: Imagine you stumble upon a new clue that's not on your map. Epistemic humility encourages us to embrace this new information and update our beliefs accordingly. It's like being open to changing your course if you find a better path to the treasure.

Understanding Limits: Just like our map can't show us the entire world, our knowledge has limits. Epistemic humility reminds us that there are things we don't know, and that's okay. It's like recognizing that even the best explorers can't discover everything in the world.

Listening to Others: Sometimes, fellow treasure hunters might have different maps or insights. Epistemic humility encourages us to listen to their perspectives. It's like realizing that collaborating with others can improve our chances of finding the treasure.

Avoiding Arrogance: If you brag about how perfect your map is, other treasure hunters might not want to help you. Similarly, if you act like you know everything, people might not want to share their knowledge with you. Epistemic humility advises against this arrogance.

As you navigate through life, remember the treasure hunt analogy. Stay open to new clues, be willing to admit when your map is wrong, and embrace the idea that learning and growth come from recognizing our limits and being open to the wisdom of others. That's the essence of epistemic humility.

Epistemic Injustice

"The smallest minority on earth is the individual. Those who deny individual rights cannot claim to be defenders of minorities."

Ayn Rand

Epistemic injustice is a concept in philosophy that deals with unfairness in the way people are treated when it comes to knowledge and information. It's like when you're playing a game, and someone changes the rules without telling you, putting you at a disadvantage. In the world of ideas and information, epistemic injustice is when someone doesn't get a fair chance to participate or is treated unfairly because of what others think about them.

Imagine you're in a classroom, and you have a great idea to share with the class. But when you raise your hand, the teacher ignores you and doesn't let you speak. This is a bit like epistemic injustice. It's as if the teacher doesn't think your ideas are worth hearing because of who you are, maybe because of your age, gender, or background.

There are two main types of epistemic injustice:
Testimonial and hermeneutical.

Testimonial Injustice: This happens when someone doesn't believe what you say or doesn't give your words the attention they deserve because of their prejudices. For example, if you're a young person and you're telling someone something important, but they dismiss you just because they think young people don't know much, that's testimonial injustice. It's like being silenced because of your age.

Hermeneutical Injustice: This type of injustice occurs when there are no words or concepts available to describe your experiences or identity. It's like trying to explain a new color that no one has ever seen before, but there are no words for it, so people can't understand what you're talking about. This can be frustrating and isolating.

So, why is epistemic injustice important to understand? Well, it's because when people are treated unfairly in terms of knowledge and information, it can lead to misunderstandings, discrimination, and even more unfairness. It's like a cycle that can be hard to break.

To fight against epistemic injustice, we should all try to be more open-minded and respectful of each other's ideas and experiences. This way, we can all learn and grow together, making the world a fairer and more understanding place.

Eclecticism

"Eclecticism is the philosophy of the open mind."

Paul Kurtz

Eclecticism is a philosophical term that means combining ideas or beliefs from different sources. It's like making a smoothie with various fruits to create a unique and tasty blend.

Imagine you're in a kitchen with a variety of fruits in front of you – apples, bananas, strawberries, and oranges. Each fruit represents a different idea or belief in the world of philosophy. Now, let's say you have a blender, and you want to make a delicious smoothie. Instead of just using one type of fruit, like a traditional apple smoothie, you decide to be adventurous.

You start by adding a slice of apple, representing one philosophical idea, like existentialism. Then, you toss in a banana slice, symbolizing utilitarianism. Next, you sprinkle some strawberries, standing for Stoicism, and finally, you squeeze in a bit of orange, which represents pragmatism.

In the same way, when someone practices eclecticism in philosophy, they don't stick to just one philosophical school of thought. Instead, they pick and choose ideas and concepts from different philosophies to create their way of thinking. It's a bit like being a philosophical chef, experimenting with different ingredients to find what tastes best to you.

Let's break it down a bit further. Imagine you're facing a particular life dilemma, like deciding whether to take a job in a different city or stay where you are. A strict adherent to a single philosophical school might approach this decision with a rigid mindset, applying the principles of that philosophy without considering other viewpoints.

However, an eclectic thinker would take a different approach. They would gather ideas from various philosophies that might be relevant to their situation. For example, they might consider the practical consequences (utilitarianism), reflect on their inner strength (Stoicism), weigh the immediate benefits (pragmatism), and ponder the existential meaning of their decision (existentialism).

By embracing this diverse range of philosophical ideas, the eclectic thinker creates a broader perspective. They can examine the problem from multiple angles and make a decision that feels right to them, drawing upon the wisdom of different schools of thought.

Eclecticism is like having a philosophical toolkit. Just as a handy toolbox contains a variety of tools for different tasks, eclecticism equips you with a toolbox of ideas and concepts from different philosophies that you can use to navigate the complexities of life and thought

Egoism

"If you're going to kick authority in the teeth, you might as well use two feet."

Keith Richards

Egoism is a philosophical idea that says people primarily act in their self-interest. In simpler terms, it's the belief that individuals tend to do things that benefit themselves more than others.

Imagine you have a plate of cookies, and you like cookies. Egoism suggests that most of the time, you'll want to eat those cookies because they make you happy. It's not that you don't care about others, but your main focus is on what makes you feel good.

But here's the twist: While egoism focuses on self-interest, it doesn't mean you should be selfish all the time. Most people balance their self-interest with caring for others. You might share some of those cookies from earlier with a friend because making them happy also adds to your happiness. It's a delicate balancing act between looking out for yourself and being considerate of others. Egoism is like recognizing that you have your own needs and desires, and it's okay to prioritize them, but it's also important to find a balance between what's good for you and what's good for the people around you.

It's a philosophical perspective that helps us understand why we make the choices we do in life, especially when it comes to questions of self-interest and morality.

Environmentalism

"It is an ironic habit of human beings to run faster when they have lost their way."

Rollo May

Environmentalism is a philosophy that revolves around caring for our planet and protecting the natural world. It's like being a guardian for Mother Earth, much like how you might care for your own home.

One important aspect of environmentalism is conservation. It's like preserving your favorite things in your room. Environmentalists want to protect endangered animals, save old forests, and keep our air and water clean. This way, future generations can enjoy the beauty of nature, just like you want to keep your special things in good condition.

Another aspect of environmentalism is raising awareness. It's like telling your friends and family about the importance of keeping your house clean and safe. Environmentalists want to educate people about the Earth's needs so that more and more folks join in taking care of our planet.

In a nutshell, environmentalism is like being a responsible caretaker of our shared home, Earth. It means protecting nature, reducing waste, using energy wisely, spreading the word, and making choices that help keep our planet a healthy and beautiful place for everyone, now and in the future.

So, just as you want your own home to be a happy and safe place, environmentalists want the same for our big home, Earth.

EQUIVOCATION

"You didn't kill him. He would have killed you, but you didn't kill him. So? He was stupid. If I killed everyone who was stupid, I wouldn't have time to sleep."

Tamora Pierce

Equivocation, in philosophy, is a concept that describes the misleading use of language, where a word or phrase is employed with multiple meanings, leading to confusion or deceptive reasoning.

Imagine you're planning a surprise party for your friend, Alex. You decide to ask Alex's roommate about their favorite type of music without giving away the surprise. Sneakily, you inquire, "Does Alex like rock music?" The roommate, unaware of the surprise, answers, "Yeah, Alex likes rocks, especially the shiny ones!"

Now, you, the party planner, are faced with a dilemma. The word "rock" has a dual meaning – it could refer to music or actual stones. The response, based on this ambiguity, doesn't provide the information you were seeking about Alex's musical taste. This situation mirrors the essence of equivocation.

In philosophy, equivocation often involves using a term in different senses within an argument. It's like a linguistic trapdoor; when someone uses a word with multiple meanings, it can create a slippery slope of misunderstanding or even manipulation.

Consider a scenario where someone argues, "A fast car is better than a slow car. Therefore, a fast car is morally superior." In this case, the term "better" is equivocated. While speed is relevant for cars, it doesn't translate to moral superiority. The shift in meaning leads to a flawed conclusion, much like the unexpected focus on shiny rocks instead of musical preferences in the party analogy.

Language is our primary tool for communication, but it's not immune to trickery. Equivocation emphasizes the importance of clarity in expression and understanding the context in which words are used. It's like decoding a secret message; if you're not careful, you might miss the intended meaning.

Let's delve into a more relatable example. Imagine you're negotiating with a friend about which movie to watch. They say, "I'm up for anything exciting tonight." Exciting could mean a thrilling action film to you, but your friend might be thinking of a heartwarming romance. Without clarifying the definition of "exciting," you might end up watching a movie that only one of you finds thrilling, resulting in a movie night that's not as enjoyable as it could be.

Equivocation is a bit like a puzzle – the pieces of meaning need to fit together for a clear picture. In the world of philosophy, where arguments are constructed with the building blocks of words, equivocation can be a stumbling block, leading to faulty reasoning and misunderstandings.

To avoid falling into the trap of equivocation, it's crucial to pay attention to how words are used and to seek clarification when encountering ambiguous language. Think of language as a treasure map; if the landmarks (words) are misinterpreted, you might end up at the wrong destination.

In the journey of understanding philosophy, being aware of equivocation is like wearing a pair of linguistic glasses – it helps you see through the haze of multiple meanings and ensures that the path of communication remains clear and honest. So, the next time you hear someone using a word that seems to shift its meaning, remember the slippery slope of equivocation and approach the conversation with a discerning ear.

Eudaimonia

"Those who educate children well are more to be honored than they who produce them; for these only gave them life, those the art of living well."

Aristotle

Eudaimonia is a term in philosophy that refers to the state of living a flourishing and fulfilling life. It's not just about feeling happy in a fleeting moment but involves a deeper sense of well-being and overall prosperity. In simpler terms, eudaimonia is like the rich soil that allows a plant to grow and thrive, rather than just survive.

Imagine a seed planted in good, nutrient-rich soil. The seed has the potential to become a healthy, vibrant plant with beautiful flowers or delicious fruits. The conditions of the soil, sunlight, and water collectively contribute to the well-being and flourishing of the plant. Eudaimonia is like the flourishing of this plant – a life that's not just surviving but thriving.

Now, let's break down the formal definition of eudaimonia. The word itself comes from ancient Greek, where "eu" means good, and "daimon" refers to a guiding spirit or inner force. So, eudaimonia translates to having a good guiding spirit or inner flourishing.

In philosophy, particularly in the teachings of Aristotle, eudaimonia is often associated with living a virtuous life. Virtue, in this context, doesn't just mean being morally good, but it's about developing positive character traits and habits that lead to a fulfilling life. It's like nurturing the plant with the right elements – integrity, courage, kindness, and wisdom are the nutrients that help a person grow and flourish.

Just as a plant needs the right balance of sunlight, water, and nutrients, a person aiming for eudaimonia seeks balance in life. Too much of anything – be it work, leisure, or even virtue – can be detrimental. Aristotle believed that finding the middle ground, or the "golden mean," is crucial for achieving eudaimonia. It's like watering the plant just enough, not too much or too little, to ensure optimal growth.

Another essential aspect of eudaimonia is the idea of personal growth and self-realization. It's about becoming the best version of yourself, much like a plant reaching its full potential. This involves discovering your strengths, passions, and unique qualities and using them to contribute positively to the world.

Think of it as a garden with various plants, each different and unique. They complement each other, creating a beautiful and harmonious environment. Similarly, in the pursuit of eudaimonia, individuals recognize the diversity of talents and qualities in themselves and others, fostering a sense of community and interconnectedness.

In conclusion, eudaimonia is about more than just momentary happiness – it's the flourishing and fulfillment that come from living a virtuous and balanced life. Picture yourself as that seed planted in fertile soil, growing into a strong and vibrant plant.

Just as a plant needs the right conditions to thrive, individuals seeking eudaimonia cultivate virtues, find balance, and contribute to the rich tapestry of life, creating a flourishing existence for themselves and those around them.

EVOLUTIONARY ETHICS

"The philosophers have only interpreted the world, in various ways. The point, however, is to change it."

Karl Marx

Evolutionary ethics is a branch of philosophy that explores the connection between human morality and the process of evolution. In simpler terms, it delves into how our sense of right and wrong might be influenced by our evolutionary history. To grasp this concept, imagine you are on a journey, not through physical landscapes, but through the evolving landscapes of human behavior and ethics.

Let's begin with a brief definition: Evolutionary ethics suggests that our moral instincts and principles have evolved as a result of natural selection. This means that certain moral traits and behaviors may have provided our ancestors with a survival advantage, leading to the preservation and transmission of those traits to future generations.

Now, let's embark on our journey through this philosophical landscape. Picture a vast terrain stretching back through millennia, with each era shaping the moral compass of our species.

In the early chapters of our evolutionary story, survival was the ultimate challenge. Imagine a tribe of ancient humans living in the wild. Those who cooperated, shared resources, and formed social bonds were more likely to survive. It was like a game where teamwork and loyalty were the keys to success. Over time, these cooperative behaviors became ingrained in our nature, laying the foundation for moral principles like fairness and empathy.

As our journey continues, societies become more complex. Think of this like the plot thickening in a gripping story. Now, humans have to navigate not only the immediate challenges of survival but also the intricacies of social structures. Our ancestors developed a sense of right and wrong to maintain order within groups. Picture a group of people agreeing on certain rules – a kind of social contract – to ensure everyone played by the same rules, fostering trust and cooperation.

Fast forward to the chapters where civilizations emerged. In these bustling societies, moral codes became more sophisticated. Imagine a city where trade, culture, and knowledge flourished. Here, ethical principles evolved to handle the complexities of interactions among diverse individuals. Concepts like justice and reciprocity became crucial for the functioning of these intricate social systems.

Now, consider the present-day landscape. Our journey brings us to a world connected in ways unimaginable to our ancestors. Evolutionary ethics contends that even in this technologically advanced era, our moral intuitions are still shaped by our evolutionary past. For instance, the instinct to care for our close kin can be linked to the idea that protecting our family increases the likelihood of passing on our genes – a notion deeply embedded in our evolutionary history.

In essence, evolutionary ethics is like reading a story where each chapter builds upon the last. The challenges our ancestors faced left an indelible mark on our moral landscape. It's not a rulebook handed down from above, but a narrative written by the trials and triumphs of our species.

Existential Phenomenology

"Expect everything, I always say, and the unexpected never happens."

Norton Juste

Existential phenomenology is a branch of philosophy that sounds complex, but let's break it down into simpler terms. At its core, it's all about exploring the way we experience and understand the world around us.

You're standing in front of a beautiful sunset. Existential Phenomenology would ask: "How do you experience that sunset? What thoughts and feelings does it bring up?"

Let's dive into this philosophy a bit more.

Existential: This part of the term refers to our existence, meaning our life and everything we go through. Existentialists believe that each person's life is unique and filled with individual experiences.

Phenomenology: This is a way of studying how we experience things, almost like looking at life through a magnifying glass. It's about paying close attention to our thoughts, feelings, and senses at any given moment.

Now, combine these two big words, and you get Existential Phenomenology, which is all about examining our unique experiences in life, like pieces of a puzzle.

Existential Phenomenologists like to explore questions like:

What does it mean to be alive?

How do we make choices in life?

Why do we have certain feelings or thoughts in different situations?

Imagine it like this: Life is like a big, mysterious book, and Existential Phenomenology is like a flashlight that helps us read and understand our own stories within that book.

Existential Phenomenology is all about diving deep into the sea of your thoughts and feelings, helping you understand and appreciate the unique story of your life. It's a tool for self-discovery and a way to make sense of the world around you as you grow and change.

Existential Nihilism

"I would never die for my beliefs because I might be wrong."

Bertrand Russell

Existential nihilism is a philosophical idea that suggests life lacks inherent meaning or purpose. This means that, according to existential nihilism, there's no grand or predetermined reason for our existence on this planet. It might sound a bit complex at first, but think of it like this: Imagine life as a big, blank canvas, and it's up to each of us to decide what kind of picture we want to paint on it.

Now, let's break this down further. In many games, there's a clear goal or mission you need to accomplish, like rescuing a princess or defeating a monster. This goal gives your actions in the game a sense of purpose. But what if you started a game, and there was no goal, no mission, and no princess to rescue? It might be fun for a little while to explore and do random things, but after a while, you might start to wonder, "Why am I even playing this game? What's the point?"

Existential nihilism is a bit like that game with no clear goal. It's the idea that life is like an open-world game where you have the freedom to do whatever you want, but no ultimate mission or purpose is waiting for you at the end. It's up to you to create your purpose, your own goals, and your meaning in life.

Now, this can be a bit daunting because it means you have to take responsibility for your own life and decisions. You're like the artist with the blank canvas – you have the freedom to paint whatever you want, but you also have to make those choices.

Some people find this liberating. They see it as an opportunity to be creative and define their path in life. Others may find it challenging because it can be unsettling not to have a clear, predefined purpose. It's like being in a vast, open field with no map or destination in sight.

Existential nihilism doesn't mean that life is meaningless in a negative way. Instead, it encourages us to find our meaning and values. It suggests that we have the power to shape our lives and give them purpose through our choices, relationships, and the things we care about.

So, while existential nihilism might make you think, "Life doesn't come with instructions," it also reminds you that you have the incredible freedom to write your instructions, follow your path, and create your meaning in this big, open-world adventure we call life. It's like being the hero of your own story, even if the story doesn't come with a predefined ending.

Empiricism

"The cosmos is within us. We are made of star stuff. We are a way for the universe to know itself."

Carl Sagan

Empiricism is a philosophy that says our knowledge comes from our experiences. Imagine you're baking cookies for the first time. You follow a recipe step by step, mixing flour, sugar, and eggs. Now, you've never made cookies before, so you have no previous knowledge about how they should taste.

Empiricism is like tasting the dough. You rely on your senses – the taste, the texture, and maybe even the smell. This firsthand experience, your taste test, is what empiricism is all about. It's learning from direct encounters with the world.

Think of your mind as an empty cookie jar. You start with no cookies (knowledge). As you go through life, you collect cookies one by one. Each cookie represents a piece of knowledge gained from your senses and experiences. For example, when you touch something hot, like a stove, and it hurts, you learn not to touch it again. That's a cookie of knowledge about heat.

Empiricists, like John Locke, believed that our minds are like blank slates when we're born. They argue that everything we know is written on this slate through our experiences. Just as you add cookies to your jar one by one, your mind fills up with knowledge over time.

Let's explore this further with an example. Imagine you've never seen a cat before. One day, you encounter a furry creature with pointy ears, whiskers, and a tail. It purrs when you pet it, and you notice it has sharp claws. This experience adds a cat-shaped cookie to your cookie jar. You now know what a cat is like.

Now, let's say you encounter a different furry creature, but this one barks wags its tail and has floppy ears. You notice it doesn't have sharp claws like the previous creature. You add a dog-shaped cookie to your jar. You can tell the difference between a cat and a dog because of your direct experiences.

Empiricism also emphasizes that knowledge gained through the senses is the most reliable kind. It values observation, experimentation, and evidence. In the world of science, for instance, scientists gather data through experiments and observations to build their knowledge. This process aligns with the empiricist idea that knowledge is grounded in what we can see, touch, hear, smell, and taste.

Epicureanism

"Don't explain your philosophy. Embody it."

Epictetus

Epicureanism is a philosophy that teaches us to find happiness and contentment in life by focusing on simple pleasures, like enjoying good food, spending time with friends, and living in harmony with nature. Imagine it like this: You're at a picnic with your friends on a sunny day.

Now, let's break this down:

Happiness Through Simple Pleasures: Epicureanism believes that true happiness comes from enjoying the little things in life, like a delicious sandwich or a beautiful sunset. It's not about chasing after big, extravagant things.

Friends and Community: Just like at a picnic, Epicureans value spending time with friends and forming close relationships. They believe that having good friends around makes life more enjoyable and helps us through tough times.

Harmony with Nature: Imagine you're sitting in a park, surrounded by trees and flowers. Epicureans think that being in tune with nature, appreciating its beauty, and not harming it is important for a happy life. Nature can bring a sense of calm and wonder.

Avoiding Unnecessary Pain: At the picnic, you want to avoid getting sunburned or bitten by mosquitoes, right? Epicureans also believe in avoiding unnecessary pain and troubles in life. They aim to minimize physical and emotional pain.

Moderation: When you're eating at the picnic, you wouldn't want to overeat and feel sick, would you? Epicureans advocate for moderation in all things. They don't go to extremes but seek balance in life.

Absence of Fear: Imagine feeling safe and carefree at your picnic. Epicureans aim to live without unnecessary fears and anxieties. They believe that when you're content with simple pleasures, there's less room for worry.

Philosophy as a Guide: Just like you'd bring a map to navigate to your picnic spot, Epicureans use philosophy as a guide to lead a happy life. They think deeply about what truly matters and follow these principles.

So, as you go through life, remember to embrace the philosophy of Epicureanism – savor the simple pleasures, nurture friendships, stay close to nature, and seek a life of contentment and peace.

Existentialism

"Things do not change; we change."

Henry David Thoreau

Existentialism is a philosophy that revolves around the idea that each person has the freedom to define their purpose in life. It's like being the author of your own story, where you get to decide the plot and meaning.

Imagine life as an empty canvas, and you're the artist. There are no pre-set pictures or rules to follow; you're free to paint whatever you like. This means that you have the responsibility to make choices and give your life meaning. You can't blame fate or circumstances because, in existentialism, you're the one in control.

Now you might be confused, how is it different from Existential Nihilism and Existential Phenomenology? So, let's understand the difference between them with an example of painting a blank canvas.

There are no pre-set pictures or rules to follow; you're free to paint whatever you like. This means that you have the responsibility to make choices and give your life meaning. You can't blame fate or circumstances because, in existentialism, you're the one in control.

Now, let's talk about existential phenomenology. This is a bit like taking a closer look at the colors and brushstrokes you're using on your life canvas. Existential phenomenology is about examining your own experiences and feelings to understand how you create meaning. It's like analyzing your emotions, thoughts, and actions to discover what they reveal about your existence. So, while existentialism is about the freedom to paint, existential phenomenology is about examining the process of painting itself.

Existential nihilism, on the other hand, is like looking at that blank canvas and thinking it's utterly meaningless. It's the belief that life has no inherent purpose or value. Imagine feeling like everything you paint is pointless because there's no ultimate meaning to it. Existential nihilism can be a bit bleak, as it suggests that life is empty, and our choices don't matter. It's like feeling lost in a vast, indifferent universe.

Now, let's dive a bit deeper into existentialism.

Existentialism emphasizes:

Freedom: Existentialists believe that you have the freedom to make choices and shape your destiny. It's like having a wide range of colors to paint your life with, and you get to choose which ones to use.

Individuality: Existentialism celebrates your uniqueness. You're not bound by predetermined roles or rules. Instead, you're encouraged to define yourself and your values. It's like being the lead actor in your play, with no script to follow.

Responsibility: With great freedom comes great responsibility. Existentialists stress that you're responsible for your choices and their consequences. You can't blame fate or others; you're in charge of your own story. It's like being the captain of your ship, steering it through the unpredictable waters of life.

Anxiety: Existentialism acknowledges that facing these choices and responsibilities can be anxiety-inducing. It's like staring at that blank book and feeling overwhelmed by the infinite possibilities. But it also believes that embracing this anxiety can lead to personal growth and authenticity.

It's like being the artist of your masterpiece, painting the canvas of existence with the colors of your choices and experiences.

Foundationalism

"I shiver, thinking how easy it is to be totally wrong about people-to see one tiny part of them and confuse it for the whole, to see the cause and think it's the effect or vice versa."

Lauren Oliver

Foundationalism is a philosophical idea that serves as a sort of roadmap for how we can build our understanding of the world around us. At its core, foundationalism suggests that knowledge, like a sturdy building, needs a strong and unshakable foundation.

Imagine you're building a tower out of building blocks. To make sure your tower stands tall and firm, you need a solid base. This base is like the foundation of a house – it's the most crucial part, and everything else depends on it. In philosophy, foundationalism works similarly.

Now, as you build your tower, you add more blocks on top of these foundational ones. These new blocks represent more complex ideas or knowledge. However, to maintain the tower's stability, each new block must be firmly supported by the blocks beneath it. This is similar to how our beliefs about the world should be supported by our foundational beliefs.

So, let's say you have a foundational belief that "the world exists." This is a pretty solid foundation because you can't doubt that the world is real – you experience it every day. Now, you can build on this foundation with more specific beliefs like "the Earth orbits the Sun" or "water boils at 100 degrees Celsius at sea level." These ideas rely on the foundational belief that the world exists.

But here's the crucial part of foundationalism: if one of the higher blocks, like "water boils at 100 degrees Celsius," were somehow in conflict with your foundational belief that "the world exists," you'd have to reevaluate things. Just like in a building, if a block in your tower is unstable or contradictory, you might need to reconsider the whole structure.

In philosophy, if you discover a belief that conflicts with your foundational beliefs, it could mean you need to reexamine those foundational beliefs or perhaps even discard them. This process of careful evaluation and adjustment is how we build a reliable understanding of the world.

FUNCTIONALISM

"Man is always prey to his truths. Once he has admitted them, he cannot free himself from them."

Albert Camus

Functionalism is a philosophical term that explores how the mind works by comparing it to something many of us are familiar with; a smartphone. Imagine your mind as a smartphone; this analogy can help us understand functionalism better.

At its core, functionalism suggests that the mind, like a smartphone, is a complex system designed to perform various functions. Just like a phone has different apps for different tasks, your mind has different mental processes for different functions like thinking, feeling, and perceiving.

Let's break it down further:-

The Hardware and Software: In our analogy, the hardware of the smartphone represents your brain's physical structure. Just as a phone needs hardware to run, your brain provides the foundation for your mental processes.

Apps and Functions: Now, consider the apps on your phone. Each app serves a unique purpose, such as texting, taking pictures, or browsing the internet. Similarly, your mind has various mental functions: thinking, remembering, feeling emotions, and more.

Functional Purpose: Functionalism focuses on what these mental functions do and how they work together to help you adapt and interact with your environment. For instance, just as your phone's camera app captures images, your mind's visual function allows you to see and interpret the world around you.

Adaptation: Like a smartphone that gets updated to perform better, your mind can adapt and change its functions to cope with different situations. When you learn a new skill or acquire knowledge, it's like adding a new app to your mental toolbox.

Differences Don't Matter: Functionalism doesn't care about the physical material of the brain but rather the functions it carries out. It's like how two smartphones might be made of different materials, but they can still run the same apps if their hardware supports it. Similarly, your mind can perform the same functions as someone else's, even if your brains are different.

Consciousness: Functionalism also considers consciousness – your awareness of thoughts and feelings. Think of it like the user interface on your phone. Just as you interact with your phone's screen, your consciousness interacts with your mental processes.

Functionalism helps us understand that the mind is not a mysterious black box; it's a set of functions working together, just like the apps on your phone. And just as you can upgrade your phone by adding new apps, your mind can grow and change as you learn and experience new things. It's a practical and relatable way to explore the philosophy of the mind, even for teenagers like you.

Hedonism

"People know what they do; frequently they know why they do what they do; but what they don't know is what what they do does."

Michel Foucault

Hedonism is a philosophy that's all about seeking happiness and pleasure as the most important things in life. Imagine it like this: life is like a journey, and the destination you're aiming for is happiness.

In the world of Hedonism, the main goal is to experience as much pleasure and avoid as much pain as possible. It's like trying to have the best time you can on your journey through life.

Now this may feel very similar to Epicureanism. Hedonism and Epicureanism both revolve around pleasure, but they differ in their approach. Hedonism emphasizes seeking immediate and sensory pleasure, while Epicureanism values a more balanced and enduring happiness that comes from a tranquil and moderate life.

Let's say you have a choice between eating your favorite ice cream or doing your homework. Hedonism would suggest that you should go for the ice cream because it gives you immediate pleasure. But, Epicureanism will also remind you that you shouldn't eat ice cream all the time because too much can lead to problems, like health issues. So, you'd also need to consider the long-term consequences of your choices.

Let's focus back on Hedonism now. Hedonism also recognizes that different people find pleasure in different things. What makes one person happy might not work for someone else. So, it's a bit like customizing your journey to happiness. Some people might find joy in reading books, while others might get it from playing sports or spending time with friends.

A very good way of understanding Hedonism is by watching the movie, Wolf of Wall Street. Now, it's important to note that not everyone agrees with Hedonism. Some argue that there are more important things in life than just seeking pleasure, like doing what's morally right or pursuing meaningful goals. They believe that simply chasing pleasure can lead to a shallow and empty life.

So, in the end, Hedonism is like a guide to living a happy life by finding the right mix of pleasure and avoiding pain. It's about making choices that bring joy and living in the moment.

Hegelian dialectic

"Happiness consists in frequent repetition of pleasure."

Arthur Schopenhauer

The Hegelian Dialectic is a philosophical concept developed by German philosopher Georg Wilhelm Friedrich Hegel. It's a way of understanding how ideas evolve and develop through a process of contradiction and resolution. Hegel believed that ideas are constantly in motion, driven by conflicts and oppositions, leading to a higher, more refined understanding.

Analogy: Imagine you're trying to build a strong and tall tower out of building blocks. At first, you start with a basic idea or concept, represented by the first few blocks you place on the ground. This initial idea is like the thesis in Hegelian terms. It's your starting point, your foundation.

Now, as you add more blocks to make your tower taller, you might come across a problem. The tower becomes a bit unstable or lopsided. This instability represents the antithesis, the opposite or contradictory force to your original idea. It's the challenge or conflict that arises as you try to develop your initial concept.

Instead of giving up on your tower, Hegelian Dialectic suggests embracing this conflict. In our tower-building analogy, you don't abandon the blocks causing the imbalance. Instead, you recognize that the conflict between the blocks is an essential part of the process. It's an opportunity to reassess and refine your original idea.

So, you decide to address the instability by carefully rearranging the blocks and finding a new arrangement that overcomes the initial problem. This act of resolving the conflict and creating a more stable tower represents the synthesis in Hegelian terms. It's the harmonious resolution that emerges from the clash of opposing forces.

But the story doesn't end there. Your newly refined tower, now taller and more stable, becomes the starting point for the next round of conflict and resolution. As you continue to build, you might encounter new challenges, leading to a cycle of constant improvement and development.

In the Hegelian Dialectic, this process of thesis, antithesis, and synthesis repeats itself, each time elevating the level of understanding and refinement. It's like climbing a ladder of ideas, where each step forward involves facing and overcoming contradictions.

Application to Real Life: Let's take an example from history: the concept of freedom. Imagine a society where people initially believed in absolute freedom without any rules or regulations (thesis). Over time, challenges arose—perhaps chaos and anarchy ensued (antithesis). In response, society recognized the need for some order and established a system of laws that balanced individual freedom with social order (synthesis).

As societies evolve, the dialectical process continues. New challenges may arise, prompting a reevaluation of the existing social order and the creation of a new synthesis. This ongoing cycle represents the dynamic nature of ideas and how they progress through conflicts and resolutions.

Hermeneutic

"I don't deserve a soul, yet I still have one. I know because it hurts."

Douglas Coupland

Hermeneutics is a philosophical term that may sound complex at first, but let's break it down to unravel its essence. At its core, hermeneutics is the art and science of interpretation, especially when it comes to understanding ancient texts, cultural practices, and even our everyday conversations.

Imagine you receive a mysterious letter written in a language you've never seen before. This letter holds a crucial message that could change your life. What do you do? You become a detective of meaning, a hermeneutic explorer, trying to decipher the symbols and unravel the hidden messages within the text.

In the same way, hermeneutics is like putting on your detective hat when you encounter something that needs understanding. It's not just about reading words; it's about diving deep into the layers of meaning that may not be immediately obvious. Let's delve into how hermeneutics works using a few examples.

Think of a movie that has layers of plot twists. On the surface, you see the characters and the events, but as you dig deeper, you discover hidden meanings, symbolism, and messages woven into the scenes. Hermeneutics is akin to peeling back those layers, trying to understand the deeper significance of the story.

Now, let's bring hermeneutics into everyday life. Imagine you're having a conversation with a friend. They say something, and you listen not only to the words but also to the tone, body language, and context. Hermeneutics encourages you to interpret the message beyond the literal words, understanding the nuances that add richness to communication.

In the world of ancient texts, like deciphering an ancient scroll, hermeneutics helps scholars understand the thoughts and ideas of people who lived centuries ago. It's like reconstructing a puzzle without having all the pieces, piecing together the fragments to glimpse the wisdom of the past.

Consider a song you love; it might have lyrics that resonate with you deeply. Hermeneutics allows you to go beyond the surface and explore the emotions, experiences, and cultural influences that shaped those lyrics. It's about connecting with the song on a profound level, understanding the layers of meaning that make it more than just a sequence of notes and words.

In essence, hermeneutics is the key to unlocking the hidden treasures of meaning in various aspects of life. It encourages us to be thoughtful interpreters, inviting us to explore the depths of literature, culture, and human expression. Just like a detective deciphers clues to solve a mystery, hermeneutics empowers us to uncover the richness hidden beneath the surface of our experiences and the world around us.

Heterophenomenology

"Some people talk in their sleep. Lecturers talk while other people sleep."

Albert Camus

Heterophenomenology is a way of studying consciousness and experience, trying to understand what goes on in our minds when we think, feel, or perceive things.

Formally, Heterophenomenology is an approach in the philosophy of mind that focuses on describing and explaining conscious experiences as they are reported by individuals, without making assumptions about the underlying mechanisms of the mind. It emphasizes the importance of taking people's subjective experiences seriously and using their descriptions as a starting point for understanding consciousness.

Now, let's imagine your mind as a mysterious and intricate amusement park. This amusement park is full of rides, attractions, and shows that represent your thoughts, feelings, and perceptions. Heterophenomenology is like being a curious visitor to this amusement park, wanting to learn about each ride and show by listening to the people who have experienced them.

In this analogy, you are the philosopher, and the amusement park represents your mind. The rides and attractions symbolize your thoughts, emotions, and sensations. Heterophenomenology encourages you to approach each visitor (which is like studying each person's conscious experience) and ask them about their adventures on the rides.

Now, imagine you meet someone who just had a thrilling experience on a roller coaster. They tell you about the twists, turns, and the rush of excitement. As a Heterophenomenologist, you take their description seriously and try to understand the roller coaster ride based on what they've shared.

Here's where it gets interesting: Heterophenomenology doesn't delve into the mechanics of the roller coaster or how it operates. Instead, it focuses on the person's description of the experience. It acknowledges that different people may have different experiences on the same ride, and the goal is to respect and understand each person's perspective.

In the world of Heterophenomenology, there's no need to open up the roller coaster to see its gears and pulleys – it's more about appreciating the diverse ways people perceive and describe the ride. It's about respecting that one person might find it thrilling, while another might feel scared, and both perspectives are valid.

Applying this to the mind, Heterophenomenologist believes that by collecting and understanding people's first-hand accounts of their conscious experiences, we can gain valuable insights into the nature of consciousness itself. It's like creating a map of the amusement park based on the stories of its visitors rather than dissecting the rides to understand how they work.

Historical materialism

"Know thyself? If I knew myself, I'd run away."

Johann Wolfgang

Historical materialism is a philosophical concept that looks at the way societies develop over time, focusing on the role of material conditions in shaping human history. In simpler terms, it's like understanding how the stuff we have (or don't have) affects the way we live and how societies change.

Imagine you're building a sandcastle on the beach. The type of sand you have, the tools at your disposal, and the weather conditions all play a role in how your sandcastle turns out. Historical materialism is a bit like studying the grains of sand, the tools, and the weather to figure out why your sandcastle looks the way it does.

Now, let's break it down a bit more. Material conditions refer to the things we use to make our lives better—like technology, resources, and even the way we organize ourselves. In the sandcastle analogy, these are the sand and tools you have.

Historical materialism suggests that the way people organize their societies, like having kings or presidents, and the economic systems they adopt, like capitalism or socialism, are influenced by the materials available at a given time. Just like your choice of tools and the type of sand will affect your sandcastle.

Think of different historical periods as different moments in your sandcastle-building adventure. Maybe at first, you only have small buckets and wet sand, so your sandcastle is tiny. Later, you get bigger buckets and better tools, and your sandcastle grows. Historical materialism examines these changes over time and tries to understand why societies make certain choices based on the materials available to them.

For example, in the past, when resources were scarce, societies might have organized themselves in ways that ensured survival, even if it meant a rigid class structure. In modern times, with advanced technology and more resources, we might choose different ways of organizing our societies, like focusing on equality and individual rights.

This philosophy also considers how these choices create conflicts. Imagine if someone is hoarding all the good buckets, leaving others with only small ones. This inequality might lead to tension, just like in history when people fought over resources or rights.

So, historical materialism is like looking at the big picture of human history, and understanding that the tools and resources available shape how societies are structured. It helps us figure out why certain societies develop in specific ways, why there are conflicts, and why things change over time.

Holism

"Learning does not make one learned: there are those who have knowledge and those who have understanding. The first requires memory and the second philosophy."

Alexandre Dumas

Holism is a philosophy that views things as integrated wholes rather than just a collection of parts. It suggests that understanding the whole is more important than analyzing individual components separately. Imagine you have a puzzle – each piece by itself may not make much sense, but when you put them all together, you see the complete picture. That's a bit like holism.

In simple terms, holism emphasizes the idea that the whole is more than the sum of its parts. It's like looking at a forest. You can study each tree, each animal, and each stream separately, but to truly understand the forest, you need to appreciate how everything works together – the way the trees provide homes for animals, the animals help with seed dispersal, and the streams contribute to the overall ecosystem. Holism encourages us to consider the interconnectedness and interactions between different elements to comprehend the bigger picture.

Now, let's break this down a bit further. Imagine you're trying to understand a car. You can learn a lot by examining each part individually – the engine, the wheels, the seats, – but it's when you see how these parts work together that you truly understand the car. The engine propels the wheels, the wheels move the car, and the seats provide a place for the driver and passengers.

Holism in philosophy is a bit like stepping back and appreciating how these components come together to make a functioning whole.

In the realm of health, holism is often applied. Instead of just treating symptoms, a holistic approach to health considers the entire person – their physical, mental, and social well-being. It's like fixing not just the broken part of a machine but understanding how the different aspects of a person's life contribute to their overall health. For example, if someone has a persistent headache, a holistic approach would explore not only the physical causes but also consider factors like stress, sleep, and diet.

Holism isn't just about seeing connections; it's about recognizing that these connections create something greater than the individual elements. Think of a symphony – each instrument playing its part, but the beauty emerges when all the instruments harmonize together. Holism invites us to appreciate the symphony of life, where various elements work in concert to create a richer, more profound experience.

In education, holism suggests that learning isn't just about memorizing facts but understanding how different subjects and skills relate to each other. It's like building a puzzle where each piece represents a different subject – math, science, literature – and when you put them all together, you get a comprehensive understanding of the world.

HUMANISM

"He died that day because his body had served its purpose. His soul had done what it came to do, learned what it came to learn, and then was free to leave."

Garth Stein

Humanism is a philosophical idea that emphasizes the importance of humans and their well-being. It's like looking at life through a special lens that focuses on people and their experiences. Imagine you have a camera, but instead of capturing nature or objects, it zooms in on human beings. Humanism is like adjusting that camera to put people at the center of the picture.

At its core, humanism values things like kindness, compassion, and empathy. It encourages us to understand and appreciate each other's feelings, thoughts, and experiences. Think of it as a way of saying, "Hey, let's treat each other with respect and care because we're all in this life together."

Humanism also promotes critical thinking. It's like having a mental toolkit that helps you question things, learn, and grow. Imagine you're trying to solve a puzzle. Humanism is the idea that you should use your brain to find the pieces and figure out how they fit together.

One more thing about humanism is that it values human potential. It's like believing that every person has a unique talent or ability waiting to be discovered. Just like how a gardener cares for every plant, humanism says we should nurture each person's potential and help them bloom.

In a world where people have different beliefs and backgrounds, humanism is like a common ground where we can all meet and agree on the importance of being kind, understanding, and respectful toward one another. It's like a guiding principle that helps us navigate the complexities of life while focusing on the shared human experience.

So, if you ever hear someone talk about humanism, remember that it's about putting people first, valuing kindness, thinking critically, nurturing potential, and striving for a better world where everyone can thrive. It's like a beacon of light that reminds us to be the best versions of ourselves and to make the world a better place for all.

Hylomorphism

"I don't know why we are here, but I'm pretty sure that it is not in order to enjoy ourselves."

Ludwig Wittgenstein

Hylomorphism is a philosophical concept that dates back to ancient Greek philosophy, particularly associated with the philosopher Aristotle. The term is a combination of two Greek words: "hyle," meaning matter, and "morphe," meaning form. Together, hylomorphism suggests that everything in the physical world is a combination of both matter and form.

Now, let's break it down with a simple analogy to better understand this philosophical idea.

Imagine you have a batch of cookie dough. The dough itself represents the "matter" or the basic substance. It's gooey, shapeless, and doesn't resemble anything specific yet. Now, think of cookie cutters as the "form." These are the tools that give shape and structure to the otherwise formless dough. You can have different cookie cutters for different shapes - stars, hearts, animals, you name it.

In the world of hylomorphism, the cookie dough is like the matter, and the cookie cutter is like the form. The delicious cookies you get after using the cookie cutter represent the individual objects or things that exist in the world. So, in a nutshell, hylomorphism is saying that everything around us is like a cookie, made up of both the raw material (dough) and the specific shape or form (cookie cutter).

Let's dive a bit deeper into this concept. According to hylomorphism, the matter and form are inseparable. You can't have a cookie without both the dough and the cookie cutter. In the same way, you can't have a chair without the wood or metal (matter) and the design or structure (form). The two elements work together to create what we recognize as a particular object.

Now, think about a tree. The matter of the tree is the soil, water, and nutrients that it absorbs. The form is the unique structure of branches, leaves, and roots that make it a tree and not, say, a bush. Every living and non-living thing, according to hylomorphism, has this duality of matter and form.

What makes hylomorphism interesting is that it goes beyond the surface level. It suggests that the form of something isn't just its physical appearance but also its purpose and function. Going back to our cookie analogy, a star-shaped cookie cutter isn't just about the appearance of the cookie; it also determines the cookie's purpose (to be a star-shaped treat).

In the same way, hylomorphism argues that the form of an object is tied to its function and purpose. A chair isn't just a random arrangement of matter; its form is designed to serve the purpose of providing a seat. This connection between matter, form, and purpose is a fundamental aspect of hylomorphism.

IMPERATIVE

"If it turns out that there is a God...the worst that you can say about him is that basically, he's an underachiever."

Woody Allen

In philosophy, an imperative is a command or a directive that expresses a necessity to perform a certain action. Imperatives are fundamental in ethical and moral discussions, guiding individuals on what they ought to do. These commands play a crucial role in shaping our understanding of responsibility, duty, and morality.

Imagine you're the captain of a spaceship navigating through the vastness of the cosmos. Your spaceship is equipped with a sophisticated Artificial Intelligence system that issues commands for optimal functioning. These commands are like imperatives in philosophy—they guide the actions of the spaceship and ensure it stays on course, avoiding collisions with celestial bodies and navigating through cosmic challenges.

Explanation

Philosophically, imperatives are like guiding principles that tell us what we should do in various situations. They are the moral compass that helps us navigate the complexities of ethical decision-making. To understand imperatives better, let's break them down into two main types: categorical and hypothetical.

Categorical Imperatives

A categorical imperative is a universal command that applies to everyone, regardless of personal desires or circumstances. It's like a rule that everyone must follow simply because it's the right thing to do. Think of it as a navigational rule for your spaceship that applies across the entire universe. For example, "Do not harm innocent beings" is a categorical imperative—it's a rule that holds in all situations.

Hypothetical Imperatives

On the other hand, hypothetical imperatives are like conditional commands. They depend on specific conditions or goals. If you want to achieve a particular outcome, you should follow these commands. In our spaceship analogy, this would be like receiving instructions based on your specific mission. For instance, "If you want to reach Planet X, adjust your trajectory accordingly" is a hypothetical imperative—it guides your actions based on your specific goal.

Understanding imperatives is crucial for ethical reasoning. They help us navigate the complex space of moral decision-making by providing clear directives. Just as the spaceship's AI ensures a safe journey through the cosmos, imperatives guide us through the moral complexities of life, helping us make decisions that align with what is considered right or good.

Consider the analogy in your own life. You might encounter situations where you face moral dilemmas—decisions that require careful consideration of what is ethically right.

Imperatives act as your guiding principles, helping you make choices that contribute to your personal growth and the wellbeing of those around you.

Ideal Observer Theory

"The highest activity a human being can attain is learning for understanding, because to understand is to be free."

Baruch Spinoza

Ideal Observer Theory is a philosophical concept that tries to understand morality and ethics. It's like imagining the perfect judge to decide what is right and wrong.

Imagine you're in a game, and you want to know the rules to play fairly. You might think, "What if there was a super-wise, super-fair referee who knows all the rules perfectly?" That's the idea behind the Ideal Observer Theory.

In this theory, we create an imaginary observer, this super-wise, super-fair referee, who knows everything about ethics and morality. This observer doesn't have personal biases, emotions, or opinions. They are like robots programmed only to know what is morally right or wrong.

Now, how does this imaginary observer help us in understanding ethics? Well, think of it this way: when we face ethical dilemmas in real life, like whether it's okay to lie or steal, we can ask ourselves, "What would this super-wise, super-fair observer say?"

This helps us make decisions based on what's morally right, rather than just what we want or what society says. It's like having a moral compass that always points to the right thing to do.

However, there are some challenges with this theory. First, we can never truly know what this ideal observer would say because it's just an imaginary concept. Second, people have different ideas about what's morally right and wrong, so the ideal observer might not give the same answer to everyone.

Imagine if you and your friend asked the ideal observer about sharing your toys. The ideal observer might say sharing is the right thing to do. But if your friend asks the same question, they might get the same answer. So, the ideal observer doesn't always solve moral dilemmas for everyone.

However, despite these challenges, Ideal Observer Theory encourages us to think more deeply about ethics. It reminds us to consider what's morally right, not just what's easy or convenient. It's like having a moral superhero to guide us, even though we can never fully know what they'd say.

IDEALISM

"The only thing that makes life possible is permanent, intolerable uncertainty: not knowing what comes next."

Ursula K. Le Guin

Idealism is a philosophy that suggests that the mind and our ideas are more real and fundamental than the physical world around us. In other words, it places a strong emphasis on the power of our thoughts and perceptions.

For example, In a game, you control a character who explores a virtual world filled with objects, landscapes, and other characters. Now, think about the fact that everything you see and interact with in the game only exists because it's programmed into the game's code. The trees, the buildings, even your character—they're all just a bunch of 1s and 0s in the computer's memory.

In this analogy, the video game represents the physical world, and the code that makes everything in the game exists represents the ideas in the mind of an idealist philosopher.

So, in a nutshell, idealism is like saying that our thoughts and ideas are the driving force behind the physical world, much like the code in a video game is responsible for everything you experience in the game. It challenges us to think about the profound impact our minds and perceptions have on the reality we encounter every day.

While not everyone subscribes to this philosophy, it's a fascinating way to explore the relationship between our thoughts and the world around us.

Individualism

"I was never aware of any other option but to question everything."

Noam Chomsky

Individualism is a philosophy that's all about celebrating and valuing the uniqueness of each person. It's like appreciating the diverse flavors in an ice cream parlor.

Each flavor is unique, just like people are. Some folks prefer chocolate, others go crazy for strawberries, and some might even love the adventurous taste of mint chocolate chip.

Individualism is about recognizing that each person is like a different ice cream flavor. It's the idea that people have their thoughts, feelings, talents, and dreams, just like how each ice cream flavor has its taste and appeal.

Here's a more concrete way to understand individualism

Freedom: Individualism is like having the freedom to choose the toppings for your ice cream. Some people might like sprinkles, while others prefer whipped cream. Just like that, individualism says that each person should have the freedom to make choices in their life, as long as those choices don't harm others.

Respect: Imagine you're in the ice cream shop, and someone picks a flavor you don't like. Individualism means respecting their choice, even if it's different from yours. It's about recognizing that people have the right to their own opinions and beliefs.

Unique Talents: Think about how some ice cream flavors are known for their special ingredients or toppings. Individualism celebrates the unique talents and skills that each person brings to the table. Just like how some ice cream flavors stand out because of their special ingredients, people can shine because of their unique abilities.

Equality: In the world of ice cream, every flavor gets a fair shot at being enjoyed. In an individualistic society, the idea is that everyone should have equal opportunities, regardless of things like their background or where they come from. It's about giving everyone a fair chance to create their own "flavor" of life.

So, in a nutshell, individualism is like savoring the diversity of ice cream flavors in an ice cream shop, where everyone gets to choose their favorite without judgment.

Indeterminacy

"I was never aware of any other option but to question everything."

Noam Chomsky

Indeterminacy in philosophy refers to the concept that certain aspects of reality, particularly in the realms of quantum mechanics and existential philosophy, are inherently unpredictable or unknowable. It suggests that there are inherent limits to our ability to precisely determine or predict certain events or states.

Imagine you have a crystal ball, and you're trying to predict the outcome of a game. In a deterministic world, the future is like a well-scripted movie where every scene is carefully planned, and you can predict the ending by connecting the dots. However, the concept of indeterminacy is like having a cloudy crystal ball. It's as if the future is shrouded in mist, making it impossible to see every detail.

Now, let's break this down further.

The Quantum Mystery: In the microscopic world of quantum mechanics, particles can be in multiple states at once. It's like a tiny coin spinning in the air, showing heads and tails simultaneously until it lands. Before it lands, we can't predict if it will be heads or tails. This inherent uncertainty at the quantum level is an example of indeterminacy.

Think of it like trying to catch fireflies in a jar. The more you try to pinpoint the location of a single firefly, the more elusive it becomes. Similarly, in the quantum realm, the more precisely we try to measure certain properties of particles, the more other properties become uncertain.

The Human Puzzle: Indeterminacy also plays a role in human existence. Imagine your life as a giant puzzle. In a deterministic world, every piece fits perfectly, and you can see the complete picture in advance. However, life often feels more like a puzzle with missing pieces.

You might decide to pursue a certain career, only to discover unexpected challenges and opportunities along the way. Relationships, too, are influenced by indeterminacy. People change, circumstances evolve, and the future of a relationship isn't always clear-cut.

Picture a road trip where you have a map, but the road ahead is filled with twists and turns. You can plan your route, but unexpected detours and scenic surprises are part of the journey. This unpredictability is a bit like the indeterminacy of life – we navigate through uncertainties, adapting as we go.

Embracing Uncertainty: Indeterminacy challenges us to embrace uncertainty rather than fear it. It's a reminder that life is an ever-changing, dynamic experience. Instead of feeling anxious about the unknown, consider it an invitation to explore, learn, and adapt.

Think of life as a blank canvas. In a deterministic world, every stroke would have a predetermined place. But in an indeterminate reality, you have the freedom to create your masterpiece. The uncertainty allows for spontaneity, creativity, and the excitement of discovering new possibilities.

Inductive Reasoning

"Man is a mystery. It needs to be unraveled, and if you spend your whole life unraveling it, don't say that you've wasted time. I am studying that mystery because I want to be a human being."

Fyodor Dostoevsky

Inductive reasoning is a type of thinking where we make generalizations based on specific observations or evidence. It involves moving from specific instances to broader conclusions. Unlike deductive reasoning, which starts with general principles and applies them to specific situations, inductive reasoning builds generalizations from specific examples.

Analogy

The Puzzle of Patterns

Imagine you are given a puzzle—a mysterious jigsaw with no picture on the box. As you begin to put the pieces together, you notice certain patterns emerging. Some pieces have similar colors or shapes, and as you connect them, you start to see the bigger picture forming. Inductive reasoning is a bit like solving this puzzle; it's about recognizing patterns in the pieces of information you have and using those patterns to make educated guesses about the whole picture.

Breaking it Down

Piecing Together Knowledge

In the world of inductive reasoning, every observation is a piece of the puzzle. Let's say you observe that every time you wear your lucky socks, your favorite team wins. This is a specific instance—wearing the lucky socks—and a specific outcome—your team winning. Now, you begin to collect more instances: every game you wear those socks, your team emerges victorious.

As you gather more pieces of the puzzle, you start to see a pattern forming. The pattern is the key. It's not just one or two instances; it's a consistent connection between wearing the lucky socks and your team winning. Inductive reasoning kicks in when you make the leap from these specific instances to a generalization: "Wearing my lucky socks brings good luck to my team."

The Puzzle's Limitations

Watch for Missing Pieces

While inductive reasoning is a powerful tool for unraveling patterns, it comes with a cautionary note. Imagine you're still working on that puzzle, and you notice that all the pieces you've connected so far are shades of blue. It would be a mistake to assume the entire picture is blue without considering the possibility of missing pieces that might introduce other colors.

Similarly, in inductive reasoning, it's important to be aware of potential missing pieces of information. Just because your team wins every time you wear your lucky socks doesn't mean the socks are the cause. There might be other factors at play—perhaps your team performs well during certain seasons, or maybe your lucky socks coincide with your team's peak performance time.

Real-Life Application

From Puzzles to Predictions

Inductive reasoning isn't just about solving puzzles; it's a fundamental part of how we understand the world. Scientists use it to formulate hypotheses based on repeated observations. For example, if they observe that a certain plant always grows better in sunlight, they might generalize that sunlight is essential for the growth of similar plants.

In everyday life, you use inductive reasoning when you predict outcomes based on past experiences. If every time you study for a test, you perform well, you might generalize that studying leads to good grades.

INEFFABILITY

"The seed of suffering in you may be strong but don't wait until you have no more suffering before allowing yourself to be happy."

Thich Nhat Hanh

Ineffability, in the realm of philosophy, refers to the idea that some experiences or concepts are so profound and complex that they cannot be adequately expressed or communicated through language. Essentially, it's the notion that there are things we encounter in life that transcend our ability to put them into words.

An Analogy

The Symphony of Emotions

Imagine attending a concert featuring a world-renowned orchestra. As the music begins, you are enveloped in a sea of sounds that stir your emotions. The melodies, harmonies, and rhythms create a symphony of feelings within you. Now, try to describe that emotional journey to a friend who wasn't at the concert. You might find yourself stumbling over words, trying to convey the depth and richness of the experience.

In this analogy, the ineffable is like the emotional depth of the music. The feelings evoked by the orchestra are intricate and nuanced, making it challenging to capture the essence with mere words. Likewise, ineffability suggests that certain experiences, often profound or spiritual, are so intricate that our language falls short of capturing their full meaning.

Delving Deeper into Ineffability

Picture a moment when you witnessed a breathtaking sunset. The colors painted across the sky, the way the sun dipped below the horizon – it left you in awe. Now, imagine expressing that awe to someone who has never seen a sunset. You might say it was beautiful, but that word hardly captures the entire spectrum of your emotions at that moment.

In philosophy, ineffability extends beyond sunsets. It delves into realms of spirituality, existential moments, or the profound experiences that make us human. Think of falling in love, the birth of a sibling, or the loss of a loved one. These moments are so deeply personal and profound that, when we try to communicate them, words seem inadequate.

Consider a dream so vivid and surreal that, upon waking, you struggle to put it into words. The dream world, like the ineffable, operates beyond the boundaries of language. It's an intricate tapestry of emotions, images, and sensations that slip away as language attempts to grasp them.

Why is Ineffability Important?

Understanding ineffability challenges us to appreciate the limits of language. It encourages humility in acknowledging that not everything can be neatly packaged into words. This concept invites us to explore alternative means of expression, such as art, music, or even shared silence.

Ineffability also plays a crucial role in spirituality and mysticism. Many religious and spiritual traditions assert that divine or transcendent experiences cannot be fully articulated. It adds an element of mystery and reverence to our encounters with the profound aspects of existence.

Infinite regress

"The menu is not the meal."

Alan Watts

In philosophy, the term "infinite regress" refers to a situation where a chain of reasoning or justification goes on endlessly, with no ultimate or foundational point. It's like a never-ending series of "why" questions where each answer leads to another question, forming an infinite loop without a clear resolution.

Imagine you're in a conversation with a friend, and you ask them, "Why do you believe this is true?" Your friend responds, "Because of X." Now, you naturally ask, "Well, why is X true?" Your friend replies with Y, but once again, you inquire, "But why is Y true?" This process continues indefinitely, creating an unending chain of explanations.

To simplify, let's use the analogy of a child's curiosity. Suppose a young sibling sees a toy car on the table and asks, "Why is the car there?" You might answer, "Because I put it there." The child, not satisfied, persists with another "why": "Why did you put it there?" You explain, "Because I wanted to keep it safe." Yet, the child's curiosity persists: "But why did you want to keep it safe?" This cycle could continue endlessly, with the child asking "why" at each step, and you providing reasons but never reaching a point where the questioning stops.

In philosophy, infinite regress becomes a concern when we're trying to establish the foundation or justification for a belief, argument, or concept. If every reason given leads to another reason, and this chain never terminates with a foundational, self-evident truth, it raises the question of whether we can ever truly justify our beliefs.

To illustrate this more abstractly, imagine building a tower of blocks. Each block represents a reason or justification for a belief. If there's no solid block at the base, and you keep stacking blocks endlessly, the tower becomes precarious and may collapse. In philosophy, the fear is that without a foundational, self-evident truth or belief, the entire structure of our knowledge and understanding may lack stability.

One famous example of infinite regress is found in the "turtles all the way down" anecdote. Picture a person claiming that the Earth rests on the back of a giant turtle. When asked what the turtle stands on, the response is "Another turtle." This continues ad infinitum, with turtles supporting each other, creating a never-ending chain. In this scenario, there's no ultimate support or foundation—it's turtles down.

Philosophers use the concept of infinite regress to challenge certain arguments or beliefs. If we can't find a solid foundation or endpoint in our reasoning, it raises doubts about the reliability and validity of our conclusions. It encourages us to seek foundational principles or axioms that can serve as the stable base for our understanding of the world, preventing the tower of knowledge from collapsing into an endless loop of "whys."

INHERENCE

"Take it moment by moment, and you will find that we are all, as I've said before, bugs in amber."

Kurt Vonnegut

Inherence is a philosophical concept that refers to the way one thing is embedded or inherent in another, suggesting a close connection or dependency between the two. It is a term often used in discussions about the relationship between properties and substances. Now, let's break it down in simpler terms.

Imagine you have a delicious chocolate chip cookie. The cookie has certain qualities like its sweetness, crunchiness, and chocolate chips that make it special. In this scenario, the cookie itself is like a substance, and the qualities it possesses, such as sweetness and crunchiness, are like properties. Now, the concept of inherence comes into play when we think about how these properties are essentially part of the cookie.

In formal terms, inherence can be defined as the relationship between a property and the object that possesses that property. It's like saying, "Hey, sweetness, crunchiness, and chocolatey goodness are not floating around independently; they are right there, part and parcel of this scrumptious cookie."

To make this idea even clearer, let's delve into a simple analogy involving your favorite pair of sneakers. Think of your sneakers as the substance, and their color, comfort, and style as properties.

The inherence here is the way those properties are woven into the sneakers, making them what they are.

So, when we talk about inherence in philosophy, we're essentially examining how certain characteristics or properties are an integral part of the very nature or existence of something. It's like looking at your sneakers and acknowledging that their color and comfort are not detachable; they are ingrained in the sneakers themselves.

Now, let's take this concept a bit further. Consider a tree in a lush forest. The tree has properties like height, leafiness, and perhaps a few chirping birds resting on its branches. In this case, inherence tells us that these properties are not random accessories but are deeply rooted in the essence of the tree. It's as if the tree wears its properties like a badge of honor, and they are inseparable from its identity.

Philosophers use the term inherence to explore the relationship between the essential qualities of things and the things themselves. It's like studying the DNA of existence, understanding how certain characteristics are not just casually associated but are fundamentally intertwined with the very being of an object or a concept.

In everyday terms, think of inherence as the glue that binds a thing to its defining features. It's what makes your pizza undeniably cheesy, your favorite song irresistibly catchy, and your friend's jokes consistently hilarious—they are not accidental add-ons but are deeply embedded in the very fabric of what they are.

Instrumentalism

"If you place your head in a lion's mouth, then you cannot complain one day if he happens to bite it off."

Agatha Christie

Instrumentalism is a philosophy that may sound a bit complex at first, but I'll break it down for you in a simple way.

Instrumentalism is a philosophy that suggests we should view scientific theories as tools or instruments to help us understand and predict the world, rather than as absolute truths about how the world is.

Think of scientific theories like a map. When you use a map to navigate, you don't expect it to be a perfect replica of the world; instead, you use it as a helpful tool to find your way around. In the same way, instrumentalism suggests that scientific theories are like maps for understanding the world.

Now, let's dive a little deeper into this idea

Imagine you're planning a road trip to a new city. You buy a map, and this map represents the city's streets, landmarks, and highways. But here's the catch: the map isn't a perfect copy of the city; it's a simplified and practical representation. It leaves out some details, like every crack in the pavement or every blade of grass. However, it includes the information you need to get from point A to point B.

In this analogy

The City: Represents the real world or reality itself. It's the vast and complex place we're trying to understand.

The Map: Represents a scientific theory. Just like the map simplifies the city, a scientific theory simplifies reality. It takes the vast complexity of the world and organizes it into a structured, understandable framework.

Your Journey: Is your quest to understand and interact with the real world. You use the map (scientific theory) as a tool to navigate this journey successfully.

Now, here's where instrumentalism comes into play

Instrumentalism says that the map (scientific theory) is not the same as the city (reality). They're different things. The map is a tool created by humans to serve a specific purpose, just like a scientific theory is a human-made tool designed to help us make sense of the world.

Instrumentalism also suggests that we shouldn't get too hung up on whether the map (theory) is a perfect representation of the city (reality). As long as the map helps us get where we want to go on our journey, it's doing its job. Similarly, as long as a scientific theory helps us make predictions and understand the world better, it's serving its purpose, even if it's not the ultimate, absolute truth. It reminds us that these theories are valuable for what they help us do and understand, rather than insisting they must perfectly mirror reality. It's a flexible and practical approach to how we think about science and knowledge.

INTENSION

"The intensional aspect of a concept reveals the depth of its meaning, encompassing the essential attributes that give it identity."

Immanuel Kant

In philosophy, the term "intention" refers to the inherent, essential characteristics or qualities that define a concept or term. It's like the DNA of an idea, encapsulating what makes it unique and distinct from other ideas. Intension is concerned with the internal nature of a concept, encompassing its defining features.

Imagine you're a pizza enthusiast, and you've just ordered your favorite pizza from the local pizzeria. Now, consider the concept of a pizza as having an "intention." This intention is like the secret recipe that makes your preferred pizza unlike any other.

Breaking Down the Analogy: The intention of a pizza includes its essential ingredients, its proportions, and the specific cooking method. These elements collectively define what makes a pizza, pizza. Similarly, in philosophy, the intention of a concept comprises the essential attributes that distinguish it from other concepts.

Now, let's delve deeper into the analogy to unravel the concept of intention.

Ingredients - Essential Characteristics: In the pizza analogy, the ingredients are crucial. The type of flour, the quality of cheese, the choice of sauce, and the toppings - these elements define the pizza's intention. Similarly, in philosophy, when we talk about the intention of a concept, we're concerned with the essential characteristics that constitute its identity.

For example, consider the concept of "triangle." The intention of this concept would include essential characteristics like having three sides, three angles, and the sum of internal angles totaling 180 degrees. These defining features make a triangle what it is.

Proportions - Defining Relations: In our pizza analogy, the proportions of ingredients matter. Too much cheese or too little sauce can alter the pizza's taste. Likewise, in philosophy, the intention of a concept involves the defining relations between its essential characteristics.

Take the concept of "parent." The intention includes the essential characteristics of having offspring and a nurturing relationship. The defining relation here is the connection between a parent and their child, emphasizing care and responsibility.

Cooking Method - Unique Essence: The cooking method in our analogy is the process that brings all the ingredients together, creating the unique essence of the pizza. Similarly, in philosophy, the intention of a concept captures its unique essence, the specific combination of essential characteristics that make it what it is.

Consider the concept of "courage." Its intention involves the essential characteristics of facing fear and taking action despite it. The unique essence of courage lies in this combination of bravery and action.

Intersubjective

"Don't only practice your art, but force your way into its secrets, for it and knowledge can raise men to the divine."

Ludwig van Beethoven

Intersubjectivity is a term in philosophy that refers to the shared understanding or mutual awareness between individuals. It's about how people connect and communicate by recognizing and acknowledging each other's perspectives, feelings, and experiences. In simpler terms, it's like a bridge that connects the islands of our minds, allowing us to share and understand each other's thoughts and emotions.

Analogy: Imagine you and your friend each have your unique island. On your island, there are different trees, animals, and landscapes that represent your thoughts, feelings, and experiences. Your friend's island has its own set of unique features. Intersubjectivity is like a magical bridge that forms between your islands, allowing you both to explore and understand the beauty and uniqueness of each other's worlds.

Explaining Intersubjectivity

Now, let's dive a bit deeper into what intersubjectivity means in our daily lives.

At its core, intersubjectivity is the ability to understand that other people have their thoughts and feelings, different from our own. It's like putting on someone else's shoes to see the world from their perspective. This isn't just about knowing that others exist; it's about truly comprehending their inner worlds.

Think about a time when you and your friend watched a movie together. After the movie, you might have discussed your favorite scenes or characters. Even if you didn't agree on everything, you could understand and appreciate each other's viewpoints. That's intersubjectivity in action. It's the shared experience of watching the same movie and being able to talk about it, even if you have different reactions.

Now, consider a disagreement you've had with a friend. Maybe it was about which video game to play or what movie to watch. In those moments, intersubjectivity becomes a bit more challenging. It's like your islands are drifting apart because you both see things differently. However, the beauty of this concept is that the bridge of intersubjectivity allows you to build understanding and find common ground.

Think of the bridge as a conversation. When you talk openly and honestly with your friend, explaining your preferences and listening to theirs, you're strengthening the bridge of intersubjectivity. It's like finding a meeting point between your islands, a place where you can appreciate each other's perspectives even if they're not identical.

Intersubjectivity isn't just important for resolving conflicts; it's crucial for building deep and meaningful connections with others. It's what makes friendships strong and relationships resilient.

When you truly grasp that others have their islands of thoughts and emotions, you become more empathetic and open-minded.

Intuitionism

"The thing about a spiral is, if you follow it inward, it never actually ends. It just keeps tightening, infinitely."

John Green

Intuitionism is a philosophy that says our moral beliefs are based on our feelings and intuitions. Instead of relying on rules or facts, intuitionists believe that what's right or wrong depends on how we feel about a situation. It's like deciding whether you like a food or not – you don't need a recipe or scientific proof; your taste buds tell you what you enjoy. You don't need a list of rules to tell you if you like it or not. Your taste buds and feelings will guide your decision. Intuitionism is kind of like that but for moral choices.

In moral situations, intuitionists trust their "moral taste buds." They believe that when we face a moral dilemma, our emotions and intuitions help us decide what's right or wrong. For example, if you see someone in trouble, your intuition might tell you to help them because it feels like the right thing to do.

Intuitionists don't think there's one universal set of moral rules that fits all situations. Instead, they believe that what's morally right can vary from person to person and situation to situation. Just like how some people love spicy food while others can't handle it, moral judgments can differ from one person to another.

But here's where it gets interesting. Intuitionists don't just rely on any feeling. They believe in "moral intuition," which is like your internal compass for what's right. This moral intuition isn't just any random feeling; it's shaped by our upbringing, culture, and experiences.

Think about how your taste for food can change over time. As you try new things, your taste buds can become more adventurous. Similarly, your moral intuition can evolve as you learn more about the world and interact with different people.

However, intuitionism also faces some challenges. Critics argue that relying solely on feelings can be problematic because our emotions can sometimes lead us astray. Just like how you might crave junk food even if it's not healthy, your moral intuitions might not always guide you toward the best choices.

In summary, It's a philosophy that says our feelings and intuitions play a big role in shaping our moral beliefs, and it recognizes that these feelings can vary from person to person. However, it's not without its critics, who question whether feelings alone are enough to make sound moral judgments.

IRREALISM

"A great many people think they are thinking when they are merely rearranging their prejudices."

William James

Irrealism is a philosophical term that delves into the idea that certain things we believe in or talk about might not exist in the way we think they do. In simpler terms, it questions the reality of concepts and wonders whether they are merely creations of our minds rather than concrete, objective truths.

Analogy

The Imaginary Friends of Philosophy

Imagine you're sitting in a room, and someone mentions their imaginary friend. Now, an imaginary friend is someone made up by a person's imagination. You can talk about this friend, describe their appearance, and share stories, but deep down, you know they're not real—they're a creation of your mind. Irrealism operates on a similar wavelength, but instead of imaginary friends, it questions the reality of concepts like justice, love, and even time.

Let's take a closer look at this by examining the concept of justice. We often discuss justice, argue about what is just or unjust, and build entire legal systems based on this idea. However, an irrealist would step back and wonder: Is justice a real, tangible thing, like a chair or a tree, or is it a concept we've created to make sense of societal norms? In other words, does justice exist objectively, independent of our thoughts, or is it a product of our collective imagination?

Consider time as another example. We talk about past, present, and future as if they are concrete realities. Irrealism, however, asks whether time is an actual entity or just a useful concept our minds have crafted to organize our experiences. Is the past something that exists tangibly, or is it merely a collection of memories that shape our understanding of events?

In a sense, irrealism challenges us to question the reality of the things we often take for granted. It's like peeking behind the curtain of our everyday thoughts and asking, "Are these concepts real, or are they just creations of our minds?"

To delve a bit deeper, let's explore the idea of beauty. We often say something is beautiful or ugly, assuming these qualities exist objectively. But an irrealist might propose that beauty is a subjective creation—a product of cultural influences, personal experiences, and individual perspectives. What one person finds beautiful might not resonate the same way with someone else, suggesting that beauty, in the irrealist lens, is more about personal interpretation than an inherent, universal quality.

Irrealism doesn't necessarily deny the usefulness of these concepts; instead, it invites us to ponder their nature. It's like realizing that the rules of a game only matter because we've collectively agreed they do.

The pieces on the chessboard don't possess an intrinsic purpose; we give them meaning through our shared understanding.

Karma

"The evil that is in the world almost always comes from ignorance, and good intentions may do as much harm as malevolence if they lack understanding."

Albert Camus

Karma is a concept deeply rooted in Eastern philosophy, particularly in Hinduism and Buddhism. At its core, karma is the idea that the actions we perform have consequences, shaping our present and future experiences. It's like a cosmic law of cause and effect, where what goes around comes around.

Formally, karma is the belief that the sum of a person's actions in this and previous states of existence decides their fate in future existences. In simpler terms, it suggests that the things you do, whether good or bad, will somehow come back to you.

Now, let's dive into an analogy to better understand karma. Imagine life as a vast interconnected web, where every action you take is like a thread. When you do something positive, it's as if you're weaving a bright, beautiful thread into the web. This thread not only adds to the overall beauty of the web but also becomes a part of your unique pattern.

Conversely, when you engage in negative actions, it's like weaving a darker thread into the web. This thread not only contributes to the complexity of the overall pattern but also becomes a part of your tapestry.

Now, picture this web as not just the events of your current life but extending beyond, encompassing your past and future lives. According to the concept of karma, the quality and color of the threads you weave determine the nature of your experiences in this life and the lives to come.

Positive actions create positive karma, leading to favorable experiences and circumstances. It's like planting seeds of kindness and compassion, and in return, you harvest a garden of joy and fulfillment. On the other hand, negative actions generate negative karma, resulting in challenges and obstacles. It's akin to planting seeds of harm and deceit, only to find a garden filled with thorns.

The beauty of the analogy lies in the interconnectedness of all these threads. Your actions not only influence your own life but also have a ripple effect on the entire web, affecting the experiences of those around you. This interconnectedness reinforces the importance of kindness, empathy, and understanding.

It's essential to note that karma is not about instant rewards or punishments. The consequences may not manifest immediately, and the complexities of the web mean that the relationship between actions and outcomes isn't always straightforward. It's a long-term perspective, emphasizing the importance of consistent positive behavior.

Materialism

"No single event can awaken within us a stranger whose existence we had never suspected. To live is to be slowly born."

Antoine de Saint-Exupéry

Materialism, in philosophy, is the belief that everything that exists is made up of physical matter or is a product of material processes. This means that everything around us, including ourselves, can be explained and understood in terms of physical substances and their interactions.

To illustrate materialism, imagine you have a delicious homemade pizza in front of you. Now, let's break down the idea of materialism using this analogy. At its core, materialism suggests that the pizza, in all its cheesy glory, is nothing more than a combination of physical ingredients. The crust, cheese, tomato sauce, and toppings are the building blocks. In the world of materialism, these components represent the fundamental elements of existence.

Now, consider your thoughts about the pizza – the joy of anticipating the first bite, the memories associated with the recipe, or the satisfaction of sharing it with friends. Materialism, however, challenges the notion that these thoughts have a separate, non-physical existence. Instead, it proposes that your thoughts, emotions, and consciousness are outcomes of intricate interactions among the physical components of your brain – much like the flavors merging on the pizza.

In simpler terms, materialism asserts that everything we experience, from the taste of pizza to the emotions it evokes, can be explained by understanding the physical makeup and processes involved. It's like saying the joy you feel is a result of specific chemicals and neural connections firing in your brain, just as the delicious taste of pizza is a result of the ingredients and their combination.

Now, let's dive a bit deeper. Imagine you take a microscope and zoom in on a pizza slice. Materialism invites us to explore the microscopic world, revealing the atoms and molecules that compose each ingredient. Just as the pizza's taste emerges from the arrangement of these tiny particles, materialism suggests that the complexity of our experiences arises from the intricate dance of atoms and molecules in the physical universe.

In essence, materialism is like looking at the world through the lens of physicality – seeing everything as interconnected and grounded in the tangible, whether it's the gooey cheese on your pizza or the thoughts swirling in your mind. It's a philosophy that seeks to unravel the mysteries of existence by delving into the intricate details of the physical world around us.

Machiavellianism

"One who deceives will always find those who allow themselves to be deceived."

Niccolò Machiavelli

Machiavellianism is a term derived from the writings of the Renaissance political philosopher Niccolò Machiavelli. In simple terms, Machiavellianism refers to a set of ideas and strategies that prioritize the pursuit of power and success, often at the expense of ethical considerations. Imagine it as a sort of political chess game where players are willing to make cunning moves to achieve their goals, even if it means bending or breaking the rules.

Now, let's break down this concept further. At its core, Machiavellianism is about being strategic and pragmatic in the pursuit of one's ambitions. It's like playing a game where the goal is to win at any cost, and the players are not bound by traditional notions of fairness or morality.

Think of it this way: imagine you are in a school competition where the ultimate prize is a prestigious scholarship. In a fair and ideal world, everyone would compete based on their skills and talents. However, a Machiavellian approach would involve some participants using cunning strategies, maybe spreading rumors about their competitors or forming alliances to eliminate strong opponents.

In Machiavellian thinking, the end justifies the means. If winning that scholarship is your ultimate goal, then, according to this philosophy, it might be acceptable to employ less-than-honest tactics. This doesn't mean everyone should adopt a Machiavellian mindset, but it's important to understand it as a perspective that exists in the realm of strategy and power dynamics.

Machiavelli, in his famous work "The Prince," explored the idea that leaders should be pragmatic and flexible, willing to use any means necessary to achieve and maintain power. He believed that leaders should focus on the practical aspects of governance rather than being bound by moral constraints.

In our analogy of the school competition, a Machiavellian participant might be someone who carefully plans their moves, forms strategic alliances, and is not afraid to use deception to get ahead. They might argue that the scholarship is so crucial for their future that taking a more ruthless approach is justified.

However, it's essential to note that Machiavellianism is not universally praised. Many people believe in the importance of ethical behavior, fairness, and honesty, even in the pursuit of success. The debate around Machiavellianism often revolves around the balance between achieving goals and maintaining a sense of morality.

Necessitarianism

"The end may justify the means as long as there is something that justifies the end."

Leon Trotsky

Necessitarianism is a philosophical term that suggests everything in the universe is necessary and could not have happened any other way. In other words, it's the idea that every event, every action, and every outcome is determined by prior events in such a way that there's only one possible course of events. Picture it like a chain reaction where each domino falls in a specific sequence, and once you set it in motion, there's only one way it can unfold.

Now, let's dive a bit deeper into this concept. Imagine you have a super-duper smart robot, let's call it Robo-Logic, that knows everything about the world. This robot knows every detail about every tiny particle, every force, and every interaction in the universe. It's like having a cosmic supercomputer that can predict everything that will happen.

Necessitarianism is like saying that if Robo-Logic knew the position and speed of every particle in the universe at a particular moment, it could tell you exactly how everything will play out in the future. It's as if the whole universe is a giant clock, ticking away in a predetermined manner.

Now, you might be thinking, "Wait, do we not have any control over our choices or actions?" Well, that's where it gets a bit tricky. Necessitarianism suggests that even our choices and actions are part of this predetermined sequence of events. It's like saying that when you decide to eat a chocolate chip cookie instead of a brownie, it was already determined by the way things were set up from the beginning of time.

Let's break it down further. Imagine you're playing a video game with a storyline. In this game, the characters have their own choices, but the game designer has already decided the possible outcomes based on those choices. Necessitarianism is like saying our lives are like that pre-designed video game. The choices we make may feel real to us, but in the grand scheme of things, they were already programmed into the game of life.

This idea can be a bit mind-boggling because it challenges the notion of free will—the idea that we have the power to make choices independent of any external influences. Necessitarianism, on the other hand, suggests that every choice we make is just the next domino falling in a long line of events that was set up from the very beginning.

It's essential to note that not everyone agrees with this philosophy. Some argue that it takes away the meaning of our choices and the responsibility we feel for our actions. Others think it's a fascinating way to look at the universe as a complex, interconnected system.

Neo-Kantianism

"Doing nothing is better than being busy doing nothing."

Lao Tzu

Neo-Kantianism is a philosophical movement that emerged in the late 19th and early 20th centuries as a reinterpretation and development of Immanuel Kant's ideas. At its core, it seeks to explore and refine Kant's philosophy by addressing perceived limitations and applying his principles to various areas of human thought and experience.

Analogy

The Invisible Playground

Imagine a playground with invisible boundaries, where everyone plays according to certain rules. Now, think of Immanuel Kant as the architect of this unique playground. He set up the rules to ensure fairness, equality, and respect for everyone playing. Neo-Kantianism is like the next generation of architects who, while respecting the original design, seek to enhance and adapt the playground for new games and challenges.

Explaining Neo-Kantianism

At the heart of Neo-Kantianism is a deep appreciation for Kant's original insights. Kant proposed that our knowledge of the world is shaped by our mental structures, like a pair of glasses through which we see reality. Neo-Kantians embrace this idea but ask: How can we refine and apply these concepts to understand the diverse aspects of human experience?

Let's break it down into three key areas where Neo-Kantians expanded upon Kant's ideas: science, ethics, and culture.

1. The Scientific Puzzle

Kant viewed scientific knowledge as a collaboration between our senses and mental frameworks. Neo-Kantians, however, faced a new puzzle. The scientific landscape was evolving rapidly, and they needed to adapt Kant's ideas to fit the emerging discoveries.

Imagine you have a treasure map (Kant's philosophy) guiding you through the forest of knowledge. Neo-Kantians, equipped with more advanced tools, explored new regions, adding details to the map. They respected the original path but recognized the need to update it for the evolving terrain of scientific understanding.

2. Ethical Navigation

Kant's moral philosophy emphasized the importance of acting according to universal principles, like treating others as ends in themselves rather than means to an end. Neo-Kantians took this ethical compass and faced the challenge of applying it to the complex moral dilemmas of their time.

Think of ethics as a journey, and Kant's principles as a reliable compass. Neo-Kantians found themselves in new territories where ethical questions were more intricate. They didn't discard the compass but sought ways to navigate the complexities, refining and adjusting it to guide them through the evolving landscapes of moral decision-making.

3. Cultural Mosaic

Kant's ideas touched upon the realm of culture and aesthetics, emphasizing the subjective nature of beauty and taste. Neo-Kantians recognized the richness of cultural diversity and asked how Kant's philosophy could appreciate this mosaic of human expression.

Imagine a kaleidoscope of cultural experiences. Neo-Kantians, inspired by Kant's acknowledgment of subjectivity, sought to understand and celebrate the kaleidoscopic patterns. They didn't change the fundamental idea but developed it to encompass the myriad ways different cultures express their unique beauty and values.

Nihilism

"The highest activity a human being can attain is learning for understanding, because to understand is to be free."

Baruch Spinoza

Nihilism is a philosophical belief that argues life lacks inherent meaning, purpose, or intrinsic value. In simpler terms, nihilists believe that there is no ultimate significance to our existence. Picture it like this: imagine you're playing a video game, and suddenly you realize there's no final boss, no ultimate quest, and no high score to achieve. Everything you do in the game seems ultimately pointless because there's no grand purpose or goal. Nihilism is a bit like that feeling applied to life itself.

Now, let's dive into a slightly more complex aspect – existential nihilism. While nihilism says life lacks inherent meaning, existential nihilism specifically focuses on the idea that individuals must create their own meaning in a seemingly meaningless world. It's like being handed a blank canvas and being told to paint your own masterpiece, even if the art gallery itself lacks any predefined purpose. So, existential nihilism acknowledges the overall lack of meaning but puts the responsibility on individuals to find or create their own purpose in the midst of this void.

To grasp nihilism better, consider this analogy: imagine you're given a puzzle without a picture to guide you, and the pieces seem to be random shapes with no clear connection. You might start feeling frustrated because, without a picture or purpose, the effort to solve the puzzle seems pointless. Nihilism is a bit like realizing that even if you manage to put the puzzle together, it won't reveal a meaningful image. The pieces, like life, lack inherent purpose.

Now, existential nihilism is akin to deciding to paint on those puzzle pieces. Even if the puzzle itself doesn't offer a predetermined image, you can create your own by adding meaning to each piece through your choices and actions. This is the essence of existential nihilism – acknowledging life's lack of inherent purpose but embracing the opportunity to create your own meaning.

To distinguish between nihilism and existential nihilism, think of it as the difference between realizing the puzzle has no inherent image and choosing to paint your own on the puzzle pieces. Nihilism is the acknowledgment of life's lack of inherent meaning, while existential nihilism is the response – the active decision to find or create personal meaning within that void.

It's crucial to note that nihilism doesn't necessarily dictate despair or hopelessness. While it challenges traditional ideas of meaning, some individuals find liberation in the idea that they have the power to shape their own purpose. It's like being handed a pen and realizing you have the freedom to write your own story, even if the universe doesn't provide a predefined plot.

In summary, nihilism is the philosophical belief that life lacks inherent meaning, much like a puzzle without a picture. Existential nihilism, on the other hand, adds a twist – it's the idea that even in the absence of inherent meaning, individuals have the power to create their own purpose, analogous to painting on the puzzle pieces. So, whether you see life as a meaningless puzzle or a canvas waiting for your brushstrokes, nihilism challenges us to grapple with the concept of meaning in our existence.

Objectivism

"Whereof one cannot speak, thereof one must be silent."

Ludwig Wittgenstein

Objectivism is a philosophy that believes in a few core ideas: that reality exists independently of our thoughts, that reason is our primary means of understanding reality, and that individuals have the right to pursue their happiness through their efforts.

Imagine you're playing a video game. In this game, there are rules that the creators have set. These rules define how the game world works, what you can and cannot do, and what happens when you take certain actions. The game world has its facts and truths. Whether you believe in these rules or not, they still apply in the game.

Objectivism is a bit like that video game world. It says that there is a real world out there, just like in the game, and it operates according to certain rules. These rules are the laws of nature, the facts of science, and the principles of logic. Objectivism tells us that these rules exist independently of what we might want or believe. They're like the game's rules; they're there whether you like them or not.

Now, let's talk about the character you play in the video game. You have choices in the game, right? You can make your character do different things, explore the world, and make decisions. Objectivism says that in real life, you are like that character. You have the freedom to make choices and take action. You have the power to use your reason, which is like your game controller, to understand the world and make decisions that lead to your happiness.

Here's where it gets interesting. Objectivism argues that you have the right to pursue your happiness, just like in the game, you have the goal to win or complete a quest. It means you can follow your dreams, set goals, and work hard to achieve them. Nobody else should force you to do things you don't want to do, just like in the game, no one should control your character except you.

But, there's a catch. Just as in the game, where your character can't break the rules without consequences, Objectivism says that in real life, you can't violate the rights of others in your pursuit of happiness. Your freedom to swing your game character's sword doesn't mean you can randomly attack other players. Objectivism emphasizes individual rights but also recognizes the importance of respecting the rights of others.

Panpsychism

"Until an hour before the Devil fell, God thought him beautiful in Heaven."

Arthur Miller

Panpsychism is a philosophical view that suggests consciousness is a fundamental aspect of the universe, existing in all things, not just humans or animals. According to panpsychism, everything, from rocks to trees, possesses some form of consciousness or mental properties.

Imagine the universe as a grand symphony, where each celestial body and every atom contributes to the harmonious melody of existence. In panpsychism, consciousness is like the music that permeates every note and resonates through the cosmic orchestra.

Unveiling Panpsychism: At first glance, the idea that even inanimate objects might have some level of consciousness may sound peculiar. We often associate consciousness with living beings, especially humans and animals. However, panpsychism challenges this common belief by proposing that consciousness is not exclusive to biological entities but is an inherent feature of the universe itself.

Let's break it down into simpler terms.

Consciousness Beyond Living Beings: Think of a rock. To most, a rock seems lifeless, a mere part of the landscape. However, panpsychism invites us to consider that, in its way, the rock might possess a basic form of consciousness. This doesn't mean the rock thinks or feels as we do, but rather it suggests that there is a fundamental aspect of awareness inherent in its existence.

Atoms as Cosmic Thoughts: Now, let's zoom in to the microscopic world of atoms. According to panpsychism, even these tiny building blocks of matter could have a form of consciousness. Picture atoms as the cosmic thoughts that make up the vast symphony of the universe. Each atom, like a musical note, contributes its unique essence to the composition of existence.

Holistic Consciousness: Panpsychism proposes a holistic view of consciousness, wherein the entire cosmos is interconnected through a universal mind. Just as individual instruments in an orchestra create a collective masterpiece, every entity, animate or inanimate, contributes to the cosmic consciousness.

Critters and Crystals: To understand this concept better, think about a cat and a crystal. In our common understanding, the cat is conscious because it exhibits behaviors, emotions, and awareness. On the other hand, a crystal seems lifeless. Panpsychism challenges this distinction by suggesting that both the cat and the crystal participate in the grand cosmic consciousness, albeit in different ways.

The cat's consciousness is more intricate and dynamic, involving thoughts, sensations, and experiences. In contrast, the crystal's consciousness, according to panpsychism, might be more rudimentary, akin to a simple, constant vibration or resonance.

A Cosmic Dance: Panpsychism envisions the universe as a continuous dance of consciousness. Every element, from the swirling galaxies to the tiniest particles, contributes its unique steps to the choreography of existence. This philosophy encourages us to broaden our perspective, inviting us to appreciate the interconnectedness of all things in the cosmic dance of consciousness.

Phenomenology

"Even the finest sword plunged into salt water will eventually rust."

Sun Tzu

Phenomenology is a philosophical term that might sound complex, but we can break it down to understand it better. In simple terms, phenomenology is all about exploring and understanding the way we experience the world around us. Let's dive into it.

Phenomenology comes from the word "phenomenon," which refers to anything that we can experience, like seeing a beautiful sunset, feeling the warmth of a hug, or even thinking about your favorite ice cream flavor. Now, think of your mind as a detective, and the world is the big mystery it's trying to solve.

Imagine you're trying to describe a delicious pizza you've just eaten to a friend who has never tasted pizza before. You'd use words to explain how it looked, how it smelled, the taste of the cheese, and the feeling of each bite in your mouth. You're describing your experience of eating the pizza. This is very similar to what phenomenology does, but instead of pizza, it's about understanding every experience we have.

Now, here's a key idea in phenomenology: it tries to get to the heart of our experiences without jumping to conclusions or bringing in preconceived ideas. It's like being a curious scientist, starting with a blank slate and carefully observing everything.

Think of your mind as a camera that captures every detail of your experiences. But here's the twist: it doesn't just capture what you see, hear, or feel. It also looks at how you interpret those experiences. So, phenomenologists don't just say, "I see a tree." They say, "I see a tall, green tree, and it makes me feel peaceful."

Now, why is this important? Because different people might have different feelings when they see the same tree. Someone who loves nature might feel happiness, while someone afraid of heights might feel anxious. Phenomenology helps us understand that our experiences are personal and unique.

Here's another way to look at it: imagine you and your friend watching the same movie. Afterward, you both talk about it. Your friend might say it was the most exciting movie ever, while you found it a bit boring. That's because your experiences and interpretations are different. Phenomenology helps us respect those differences and understand why they happen.

In essence, phenomenology is like taking a magnifying glass to our everyday experiences, whether it's savoring pizza or watching a movie, and trying to understand them deeply. It reminds us that each person's perspective is valuable and worthy of exploration.

Postmodernism

"Death, therefore, the most awful of evils, is nothing to us, seeing that, when we are, death is not come, and, when death is come, we are not."

Epicurus

Postmodernism is a philosophy that challenges the way we think about and understand the world. At its core, it questions the idea that there is one single, absolute truth or reality. Instead, it suggests that truth and reality are more like a kaleidoscope – they can look different from different angles, and they can change over time.

Suppose you're looking at a beautiful piece of abstract art. Different people might see different things in it. One person might see a bird, another a flower, and yet another might see something completely different. In traditional thinking, there would be one correct answer about what the painting represents. But in a postmodern view, all these interpretations are valid because they reflect the unique perspectives and experiences of the individuals looking at the art.

Now, let's apply this idea to how we understand the world. Postmodernism says that our understanding of reality is shaped by our culture, our history, and our personal experiences. This means that what we consider "true" or "real" can vary from person to person and from one time period to another.

Think about history books. In the past, history was often written from the perspective of those in power – kings, conquerors, and rulers. But postmodernism asks us to question this. It says, "What about the stories of ordinary people, of women, of minorities? Aren't their experiences and truths just as important?" So, postmodernism encourages us to look at history from different viewpoints and to recognize that there are many "truths" hidden within it.

Postmodernism also challenges the idea of "grand narratives." These are big, overarching stories or theories that try to explain everything. Postmodernists argue that these grand narratives are limiting because they don't take into account the complexity and diversity of human experience. Instead, they suggest that we should embrace "mini-narratives" – smaller, more personal stories that reflect individual perspectives.

Now, let's talk about language. Postmodernism is interested in how language shapes our understanding of reality. It suggests that language is not just a tool for communication but also a way of exercising power. Words can be used to control and manipulate, and postmodernism encourages us to be critical of the language used by those in authority.

In everyday life, postmodernism challenges us to be open-minded and tolerant of different viewpoints. It asks us to be aware of our biases and to question the "truths" we take for granted. It reminds us that there are many ways of seeing the world, and that's what makes life interesting and rich.

Pantheism

"If you're trapped in the dream of the Other, you're f**ked."

Gilles Deleuze

Pantheism is a philosophy that believes that everything in the universe is divine, and this idea can be a bit like seeing the world as one big, interconnected family.

Imagine the universe as a giant puzzle, where each piece is a part of the whole. In pantheism, every piece of the puzzle represents something in the universe – whether it's a tree, a rock, a person, or even a tiny ant. Now, here's the twist: in pantheism, each of these pieces is not just a part of the puzzle; it's also the puzzle itself. Confusing, right? Let's break it down.

In many religions, people worship gods or deities who are separate from the world. These gods created the universe but exist outside of it. It's like having a toy train set, and you're the one playing with the trains, controlling them from above. You're separate from the trains, just like how gods are separate from the world in many religions.

Now, pantheism flips this idea on its head. It says that the universe itself is like the grand conductor of the train set. It's not controlled by someone else; it is the control. The universe, in pantheism, is like the magical force that makes everything happen.

Think of this puzzle as something sacred or divine. Pantheism doesn't point to a single god or deity separate from the universe. Instead, it says that the universe, with all its pieces, is what some people might call "God" or the ultimate, all-encompassing force. It's a bit like saying the universe itself is the big, amazing, and interconnected web of existence that we should respect and admire.

Pantheism doesn't have a set of rules or a specific religious text like some other belief systems. Instead, it encourages people to find their spiritual connection with the universe. It's a bit like saying, "Look around you, at the stars, the oceans, and the people you meet. They are all part of something much greater than themselves." Pantheists often feel a deep sense of awe and wonder when they contemplate the beauty and complexity of the universe.

Poststructuralism

"The real question of life after death isn't whether or not it exists, but even if it does what problem this really solves."

Ludwig Wittgenstein

Post-structuralism is a way of thinking about the world and language that suggests there are no absolute truths or fixed meanings. Instead, it explores how ideas and words are shaped by different perspectives and contexts.

Now, let's use an analogy to help you understand this better.

Imagine you're in a library, surrounded by books. Each book represents an idea or a piece of knowledge. In the past, people used to think of these books as containing all the answers, like they were the ultimate truth. But post-structuralism says, "Hold on a second, let's look closer."

The library is like a world of ideas, and each book is a belief or a way of understanding things. Before post-structuralism, people thought these books had one clear and fixed meaning, just like they thought there was one absolute truth about the world. It's like they believed there was only one way to read each book.

But post-structuralism shakes things up. It suggests that the meaning of a book (or an idea) isn't set in stone. Instead, it can change depending on who's reading it and the context in which they're reading it. So, it's like saying that the same book might mean different things to different people, or even to the same person at different times in their life.

Think about it this way: If you read a book about love when you're in a happy relationship, you might see it as a beautiful and positive thing. But if you read that same book when you're going through a tough breakup, you might interpret it very differently. The words in the book haven't changed, but your perspective and feelings have.

Post-structuralism also challenges the idea that there's one "right" way to organize the books in the library. It's like saying, "Why do we put all the science books in one section and all the poetry books in another? Who decided that?" This philosophy suggests that the categories and labels we use, whether in books or our thinking, are not fixed or universal. They can vary from culture to culture and person to person.

It's okay if this seems a bit tricky at first. Post-structuralism is like exploring a new way of looking at the world, one that challenges old assumptions and invites us to think more deeply about how we understand things.

Platonism

"I have gained this by philosophy; I do without being ordered what some are constrained to do by their fear of the law."

Aristotle

Platonism is a philosophical idea that dates back to the ancient Greek philosopher Plato. At its core, Platonism suggests that there are abstract, unchanging concepts or forms that exist independently of the physical world. These abstract forms are like perfect blueprints for everything we see around us.

Imagine you're an architect designing a house. Before you even start drawing the plans or building anything, you have a perfect idea in your mind of what the house should look like. This mental image is like Plato's abstract form. It's the ideal, unchanging concept of a house that exists in your thoughts.

Now, when you build a house, it might not be perfect. There could be imperfections or variations from your ideal mental image. That's because the physical world is full of imperfections. But your mental concept of the perfect house remains the same. It's like the unchanging abstract form of a house that all real houses are trying to imitate.

Plato believed that everything in the physical world is a flawed copy of these perfect abstract forms. So, when you see a beautiful flower, what you're seeing is a less-than-perfect imitation of the abstract form of beauty. Similarly, when you encounter a just action or a good person, they are reflections of the abstract forms of justice and goodness.

Another way to think about Platonism is through mathematics. Mathematical concepts like the number one or the Pythagorean theorem are abstract and unchanging. They exist whether or not someone is doing math. When you write down "1 + 1 = 2," you're expressing an eternal truth about the abstract concept of numbers. In this sense, mathematics is a realm of abstract forms.

Plato's idea of the physical world as a realm of imperfect copies has some profound implications. It suggests that there's a deeper, more real reality beyond what we can see and touch. It challenges us to seek knowledge and understanding of these abstract forms, which are more enduring than the ever-changing world around us.

Pragmatism

"The utility of any belief is the sole reason for its existence."

Charles Sanders Peirce

Pragmatism is a philosophy that emphasizes practicality and the real-world consequences of our actions and beliefs. In simpler terms, it's all about making practical choices based on what works best in a given situation.

In a toolbox with different tools in it. Each tool serves a specific purpose, like a hammer for pounding nails or a screwdriver for turning screws. Now, think of your beliefs and actions as tools in your mental toolbox. Pragmatism is like choosing the right tool for the job.

Let's break it down further

What's the Problem?

Imagine you have a loose doorknob. You want to fix it. This is the problem you're facing.

Choosing a Tool (Belief/Action):

In your mental toolbox, you have two beliefs:

Belief A: "I should use a wrench to tighten the doorknob."

Belief B: "I should use a screwdriver to tighten the doorknob."

Pragmatic Decision

Pragmatism says, "Which tool (belief) will solve the problem effectively?" In this case, using a wrench (Belief A) is the practical choice because it's designed for the job.

Real-World Consequences

Now, imagine you go ahead and use the screwdriver (Belief B) instead, even though it's not the right tool. What happens? The doorknob remains loose, and you might even damage it further. These are the real-world consequences of your choice.

So, pragmatism is all about choosing beliefs and actions that work best for solving real-life problems. It encourages you to be practical and consider the actual outcomes of your choices.

Now, let's apply this to life situations

Example 1: Career Choices

Imagine you're deciding on a career path. Pragmatism suggests you should consider what career will provide financial stability, job satisfaction, and growth opportunities. Instead of pursuing a dream job that offers no practical benefits, like income to support yourself, you'd choose a career that meets your real-world needs.

Example 2: Relationships

In relationships, pragmatism means choosing partners who treat you well, respect your values, and contribute positively to your life. It's about avoiding relationships that are harmful or incompatible with your goals, even if they seem exciting at first.

Example 3: Environmental Choices

When it comes to the environment, pragmatism encourages you to make choices that benefit the planet and, by extension, future generations. It means reducing waste, conserving resources, and supporting sustainable practices because these choices have practical, positive consequences for the world we live in.

Predestination

"Freedom is the only worthy goal in life. It is won by disregarding things that lie beyond our control."

Epictetus

Predestination, in philosophy, is the idea that everything that happens in the universe has already been determined or decided by some higher power or force. It's like a script for a play that has been written in advance, and all the actors (which includes us) are simply following the lines and actions laid out in that script.

In this concept, there's a belief that a divine being, fate, or some mysterious force has already decided how the entire story of existence will play out, and we're just actors following a fixed script. It's like you're playing a video game with only one path to follow, and no matter what choices you make, you'll always end up at the same conclusion because the outcome is set in stone.

Now, let's distinguish this from determinism. While predestination and determinism share similarities, they're not quite the same. Determinism also proposes that everything is predetermined, but not necessarily by a divine entity. Instead, it suggests that the laws of nature, like physics and chemistry, control everything. In this case, imagine the universe as a giant machine with all its cogs and gears working together, following strict rules.

So, the key difference is in who or what is doing the predetermining. In predestination, it's often seen as a divine being or force, while in determinism, it's the natural laws of the universe. Think of it like two different scripts for the same play—one written by a divine playwright and the other by the laws of science

To make it clearer, let's look at a simple example: getting up in the morning. In a predestination scenario, the moment you wake up at a specific time, eat a particular breakfast, and choose your clothes has all been predetermined by this higher power. You might think you're making choices, but in reality, you're just following the pre-written script.

In a deterministic world, it's as if the laws of nature dictate when you wake up. Maybe it's because of your body's internal clock, which is influenced by natural rhythms. Your choice of breakfast is determined by your taste preferences and what's available in your kitchen, following the laws of supply and demand. Even your choice of clothes might depend on the weather forecast, which is governed by atmospheric conditions.

Pre-Socratic Philosophy

"Feathers filled the small room. Our laughter kept the feathers in the air. I thought about birds. Could they fly if there wasn't someone, somewhere, laughing?"

Jonathan Safran Foer

Pre-Socratic philosophy refers to the philosophical ideas and inquiries that emerged in ancient Greece before the time of Socrates, who lived around 469-399 BCE. These early thinkers laid the groundwork for Western philosophy by exploring fundamental questions about the nature of the universe, its existence, and the underlying principles that govern reality.

Analogy: Imagine you're in a vast and mysterious forest. The Pre-Socratic philosophers are like the bold explorers who ventured into this uncharted territory, trying to understand the secrets of the trees, the animals, and the unseen forces that govern the forest. They were the first to pick up the compass and start mapping out the philosophical landscape.

Exploration of Nature: Just as our explorers in the forest examined the intricacies of the trees and the behavior of animals, the pre-Socratic philosophers focused on understanding the natural world. They were curious about the fundamental elements that make up everything around us—earth, water, air, and fire. Think of them as ancient scientists, attempting to unlock the mysteries of nature without the advanced tools we have today.

Thales, one of the earliest pre-Socratic thinkers, believed that water was the fundamental substance of the universe. It's like saying, "Everything in this forest is made of water!" just as some might claim everything is made of atoms today. These early philosophers weren't satisfied with accepting things at face value; they wanted to delve deeper into the essence of reality.

Cosmic Questions: Now, imagine our explorers gazing up at the night sky, pondering the stars and the moon. Similarly, the pre-Socratic philosophers asked profound questions about the cosmos. Anaximander, for instance, wondered about the origin and structure of the universe. He proposed the idea of an indefinite, boundless substance called the "apeiron," a concept as mysterious as the vastness of the night sky itself.

These thinkers weren't content with merely observing; they sought to grasp the underlying principles that governed the entire cosmic spectacle. It's like them trying to find the rulebook that governs the behavior of the stars and planets.

Metaphysical Musings: Picture our explorers sitting around a campfire, discussing not just the physical aspects of the forest but also abstract concepts like beauty, justice, and change. Similarly, the Pre-Socratic philosophers ventured into metaphysics—questions beyond the physical world.

Heraclitus, known for his famous saying "You cannot step into the same river twice," contemplated the nature of change. It's akin to our explorers pondering how the forest evolves, with trees growing and seasons changing. Heraclitus believed that change was fundamental to the nature of reality.

Legacy of Exploration: The explorers in our analogy, like the Pre-Socratic philosophers, left a legacy. Their maps and observations paved the way for future generations to build upon their ideas. Socrates, Plato, and Aristotle would come later, expanding and refining the philosophical landscape.

Process Theology

"Life is never made unbearable by circumstances, but only by lack of meaning and purpose."

Victor Frankl

Process theology is a philosophical idea that helps us understand how the world works and how we can think about the nature of reality. It's like looking at the world as a never-ending dance instead of a fixed and unchanging picture.

Picture a dance floor where people are constantly moving, flowing, and changing their positions. This dance never stops, and it's always evolving. This dance represents everything in the world, from people and animals to plants and even the tiniest particles.

Now, in this dance, there are two important characters: God and the world. God is like the choreographer, the one who guides the dance, and the world is the dancers. But here's the twist: in process theology, God is not a bossy choreographer who plans every move. Instead, God is part of the dance itself, dancing along with the world.

In the dance of process theology, everything is about change and interaction. The dancers (the world) are not fixed in one place; they are always moving and evolving. They interact with each other, responding to the music and the other dancers' moves. God, as the choreographer, doesn't just give orders from the sidelines but joins in the dance, making creative decisions as the dance unfolds.

One key idea in process theology is that the future is not set in stone. In traditional views, people often think that God has a predetermined plan for everything, like a script for a play. But in the dance of process theology, there's no fixed script. Instead, the future is open, and it depends on how the dance unfolds.

God in process theology doesn't force things to happen but persuades the dancers (the world) to make good choices. It's like God is a great partner in a dance, gently guiding us without taking away our freedom to move and make choices. God aims to inspire us to make the best moves, to make the dance as beautiful as possible.

Why Is This Important?

Process theology helps us make sense of a world that's always changing. It reminds us that we have a part to play in shaping the future through our choices and actions. It encourages us to be creative, make good decisions, and take responsibility for our part in the dance of life.

Quietism

"Seize the moments of happiness, love and be loved! That is the only reality in the world, all else is folly. It is the one thing we are interested in here."

Leo Tolstoy

Quietism is a philosophy that suggests we should find peace and contentment in doing nothing, rather than actively seeking change or pursuing desires.

Imagine you're in a boat on a calm lake. The water is still, and there are no waves or ripples. You're just floating, not trying to row or make any waves. This is a bit like what quietism teaches. It encourages you to be like that calm lake, finding tranquility in being still and not causing disturbances.

Now, let's dive a bit deeper into what quietism is all about.

Formal Definition

Quietism is a philosophical belief that emphasizes inner peace and stillness as the highest spiritual state. It teaches that you should accept things as they are, without trying to change or control them. Instead of pursuing desires or ambitions, quietism suggests finding contentment in the present moment and letting go of the need for external achievements.

Explanation: Think of life as a river. Many people spend their lives swimming against the current, always trying to reach something farther downstream. They set goals, work hard, and often feel stressed because they're constantly pushing against the flow of life.

Quietism, on the other hand, encourages you to float with the current. Instead of constantly striving for more, it says, "Hey, just relax and enjoy the ride." It's like taking a break from the race and finding a peaceful spot by the riverbank to rest.

Now, this doesn't mean you should never do anything or be lazy. It's more about your mindset. Quietism teaches you to let go of the need to control everything and accept that some things are beyond your control. It's about finding peace in simply being, without always chasing after something new.

Imagine you're studying for a big exam. Many students might stress out, study for hours, and worry about the outcome. But a quietist approach would be to study calmly, do your best, and accept that whatever the result, it's okay. You're not overly attached to the outcome because you've found peace in the process.

Another way to understand quietism is through meditation. When you meditate, you focus on your breath and let go of racing thoughts. You're not trying to change anything; you're just being present and peaceful. This is a lot like the quietist philosophy—it's about finding stillness within yourself.

In the busy world we live in, where we're often told to achieve more and do more, quietism offers a different perspective. It reminds us that sometimes, the most profound peace and contentment come from simply being still and accepting the world as it is, just like that calm lake where everything is serene.

Rationalism

"Life is much more successfully looked at from a single window."

F. Scott Fitzgerald

Rationalism is a philosophy that believes in the power of human reason and intellect as the primary source of knowledge and understanding. It emphasizes the importance of thinking, analyzing, and using logical thought processes to gain knowledge about the world. Think of it like having a superpower – the power of rational thinking.

Imagine your brain is like a superhero's headquarters. This superhero is called "Reason." Reason wears glasses, and those glasses are like your ability to think logically and critically. It's like having a special tool that helps you make sense of the world.

Now, let's break down rationalism further

The Power of Reason: Rationalism says that the best way to figure out things about the world is to use your brain's superpower – reason. Instead of relying on emotions or faith, rationalism encourages you to think deeply and critically. It's like using your superhero glasses to see through the fog of uncertainty.

Knowledge from Within: Rationalists believe that knowledge is something you can discover from inside yourself. It's not about looking outward or relying on external sources like tradition or authority figures. Imagine your brain as a treasure chest, and the rationalist superhero helps you unlock it to find the treasures of knowledge hidden within.

Math and Science: Rationalism loves math and science. It's like having a laboratory where you can conduct experiments and use logic to solve complex problems. For example, when you're learning about gravity, rationalism encourages you to use math and reason to understand how it works rather than just accepting it as a magical force.

Question Everything: Rationalism is all about asking questions. It's like being a detective who constantly investigates and examines ideas. Instead of taking things at face value, you use your superhero glasses to dig deeper, challenge assumptions, and seek evidence.

Skepticism: Rationalists tend to be skeptical, which means they don't believe things easily. It's like having a truth detector in your superhero headquarters. You don't accept things as true unless you have good reasons and evidence to support them.

Descartes' Famous Quote: One of the most famous rationalists, René Descartes, once said, "I think, therefore I am." This means that the act of thinking proves your existence. It's like saying, "I can doubt things, so I must exist because only a thinking being can doubt." Descartes used rationalism to start from scratch and build up his understanding of the world using reason.

Realism

"If you have reasons to love someone, you don't love them."

Slavoj Žižek

Realism in philosophy is the belief that the things we perceive and experience in the world around us are real and exist independently of our thoughts or perceptions. It suggests that there is a reality out there, and our perceptions and thoughts are attempts to understand and describe this external reality accurately.

Now, let's imagine realism using a simple analogy

Think of a movie theater. When you go to watch a movie, you see all sorts of exciting adventures, like superheroes saving the world or characters going on incredible journeys. The movie screen is like the world you see around you, full of people, objects, and events.

Realism, in philosophy, is a bit like believing that the movie on the screen represents the real world. It's saying that the adventures you see in the movie are happening in a genuine place, just like the world we live in. Even when you're not watching the movie, you believe that the characters, places, and events still exist somewhere.

So, how does this relate to philosophy? Well, in the world of ideas and thoughts, philosophers have different views about what's real.

Some think that only the things we can see, touch, and measure are real, much like believing that the movie on the screen is the only real thing. This philosophy is called materialism.

Others, like the realists, believe that there is more to reality than what we can directly perceive. They think that things like concepts, mathematical truths, and even the past and future are just as real as the physical world. It's a bit like saying the adventures of the movie characters exist even when the movie isn't playing.

Now, here's where it gets interesting: realists think that our thoughts and ideas are like the projector that shows the movie on the screen. They believe that our thoughts and ideas are ways of revealing and understanding the real world, much like how the projector brings the movie to life.

Imagine you're trying to describe the characters and events in the movie to your friend. You use words to paint a picture in their mind. In the same way, realists believe that our thoughts and ideas are like tools we use to describe and understand the real world.

Realism encourages us to explore and understand the world around us, not just what we can see and touch but also the ideas and concepts that shape our understanding of reality. It's a bit like turning on the projector of our minds to explore the grand movie of the universe, where thoughts and ideas play a crucial role in discovering the truth about our world.

Relativism

"One's life has value so long as one attributes value to the life of others, using love, friendship, and compassion."

Simone de Beauvoir

Relativism is a philosophical term that means believing that what is true or right can vary from person to person or from one situation to another. Imagine you and your friend are standing on opposite sides of a large, colorful mural. Your friend sees a beautiful butterfly painted on it, while you see a magnificent flower. Who is right? Well, that's where relativism comes in.

Formal Definition: Relativism is the idea that truth, morality, and even reality itself can be different for different people or in different situations.

Let's use an analogy to understand this better

Imagine you and your friend, Sarah, are trying to decide what the best ice cream flavor is. You say, "Chocolate is the best!" But Sarah insists, "No way, vanilla is the best!"

Now, let's think about this situation in the context of relativism. In a way, you both are right, but only for yourselves. For you, chocolate is the best because you love its rich, creamy taste. For Sarah, vanilla is the best because she enjoys its simplicity and how it goes with almost any topping.

Here's where relativism kicks in: it suggests that what's true (the best ice cream flavor in this case) can be different for different people. It acknowledges that your personal experiences, preferences, and perspectives shape your views. So, there's no one "ultimate" best ice cream flavor that applies to everyone.

Now, let's apply relativism to a more complex scenario, like ethics. Imagine there's a debate about whether lying is always wrong. Some people believe that lying is never okay, while others think there might be situations where it's justified, like telling a little white lie to spare someone's feelings.

From a relativistic point of view, both sides can have valid arguments. The idea is that the morality of lying can vary depending on the circumstances and individual beliefs. What's considered right or wrong can change from person to person or situation to situation.

It's essential to understand that relativism doesn't mean anything goes or that there are no moral standards at all. It simply recognizes that our judgments about what's true, right, or wrong can be influenced by our unique perspectives, cultural backgrounds, and personal experiences.

While relativism encourages open-mindedness and respect for diverse opinions, it also sparks important debates about whether there are any universal moral truths. Some people argue that certain ethical principles should apply to everyone, regardless of their perspectives.

In the end, relativism reminds us to consider different points of view and be aware that what seems true or right to one person might not be the same for another. It encourages thoughtful discussions and the exploration of varying beliefs while emphasizing the importance of empathy and understanding in a world where people can see things differently.

RHETORIC

"Even a soul submerged in sleep is hard at work and helps make something of the world."

Heraclitus

Rhetoric is the art of using language effectively and persuasively to communicate and convince others. It involves the skillful use of words, phrases, and techniques to influence an audience's thoughts or actions.

Consider building a Bridge of Words Imagine you are an architect tasked with constructing a bridge between two islands. Your goal is to connect these separate lands, just as rhetoric aims to bridge the gap between different minds and opinions. Now, let's break down the analogy to understand how rhetoric functions similarly.

Foundation: Ethos, Pathos, and Logos A strong bridge needs a solid foundation, and rhetoric has its foundation built on three pillars: Ethos, Pathos, and Logos.

Ethos (Credibility): Just as a reputable architect lends credibility to a bridge project, the speaker or writer establishes credibility in rhetoric. This is achieved by showcasing expertise, integrity, and a connection with the audience. Imagine the architect displaying a portfolio of successful bridges built in the past.

Pathos (Emotion): Emotions act as the mortar that holds the bridge together. Rhetoric appeals to the audience's feelings, making the message relatable and emotionally resonant. Think of the architect explaining how the bridge will reunite families separated by water, evoking a sense of joy and togetherness.

Logos (Logic): Like the structural design of a bridge, rhetoric relies on logic. It presents a clear, reasoned argument supported by evidence and facts. In our analogy, the architect uses engineering blueprints and data to prove the bridge's stability and practicality.

Construction: Devices and Strategies With the foundation laid, it's time to construct the bridge. In rhetoric, various devices and strategies are employed to enhance the effectiveness of communication.

Metaphors and Similes: These are like decorative elements on the bridge, making the language vivid and relatable. If the architect compares the bridge to a handshake, emphasizing unity, it creates a memorable image.

Repetition: Just as a well-placed support beam reinforces the structure, repeating key ideas in rhetoric strengthens the argument. Imagine the architect repeating the importance of unity and connection throughout the presentation.

Rhetorical Questions: These are like signposts on the bridge, guiding the audience's thoughts. If the architect asks, "Can we afford to remain divided?" it prompts reflection and emphasizes the urgency of the bridge.

Maintenance: Adaptation and Responsiveness A good bridge withstands changing weather conditions, and effective rhetoric adapts to different audiences and contexts.

Audience Awareness: Like checking the weather forecast, understanding the audience is crucial. A rhetorician adjusts language, tone, and examples to resonate with the specific audience, just as an architect considers the terrain and climate.

Counterarguments: Anticipating opposing views is like inspecting the bridge for potential weaknesses. By addressing counterarguments, rhetoric strengthens its position and demonstrates thorough consideration.

The Completed Bridge: Impact and Persuasion When the bridge is finished, it not only connects islands but also facilitates movement and exchange. Similarly, effective rhetoric not only communicates a message but also influences thoughts, opinions, and actions.

Empowerment: The connected islands can now thrive together, and persuasive rhetoric empowers the audience to act or think in a particular way. It inspires change and fosters understanding.

Legacy: Just as a well-built bridge stands the test of time, memorable rhetoric leaves a lasting impact. Speeches like Martin Luther King Jr.'s "I Have a Dream" oratory endure because they effectively used rhetoric to inspire and ignite change.

In summary, rhetoric is the craftsmanship of persuasive communication, constructing bridges of understanding and influence between people.

Like a skilled architect, a rhetorician uses the right materials, designs, and strategies to create a connection that withstands the tests of time and differing perspectives.

Sartrean Existentialism

"It is therefore senseless to think of complaining since nothing foreign has decided what we feel, what we live, or what we are."

Jean-Paul Sartre

Sartrean existentialism posits that existence precedes essence. In other words, unlike a chair, which has a predetermined essence (its purpose as a seat), humans do not have a predefined purpose. Instead, we exist first and then define our essence through our actions and choices. This philosophy places a profound emphasis on individual freedom, highlighting that we are not bound by any inherent human nature or external forces.

Imagine life as a blank canvas, and you are the artist holding the paintbrush. The canvas represents your existence, and the colors you choose to paint symbolize the decisions you make. Sartre would argue that you are not restricted by a predetermined picture; instead, you have the liberty to create and redefine your masterpiece through every brushstroke.

Distinguishing Sartrean Existentialism from Existentialism: Existentialism, in a broader sense, is a philosophical movement that explores individual existence, freedom, and choice. Sartrean existentialism is a specific branch, and what sets it apart is the concept of radical freedom. Sartre believed that not only are we condemned to be free, but we are also responsible for our freedom. This responsibility can be daunting, but it is the crux of Sartre's philosophy.

In a nutshell, while existentialism acknowledges the importance of choice, Sartrean existentialism takes it a step further, asserting that our freedom is absolute and that we must take full responsibility for our actions.

Freedom and Responsibility: Sartrean existentialism places a premium on individual freedom, but with great freedom comes great responsibility. Imagine having the power to shape your destiny; it's like being the captain of your ship. However, this captaincy involves not just the thrill of navigating the waters but also the responsibility of ensuring the ship reaches its destination safely. Likewise, in life, our freedom is exhilarating, but it necessitates accountability for the paths we choose.

The "Existential Dilemma" - Embracing Anxiety: Sartre introduced the concept of "existential angst" or anxiety. This is not the everyday worry about exams or social situations; it's a deeper unease about the weight of our choices and the responsibility they entail. Picture standing at a crossroads, uncertain about which path to take. The anxiety stems from the realization that you alone must decide, and your choice will shape your journey. Sartre argues that this anxiety is an integral part of our existence, and rather than shying away from it, we should confront and embrace it as a testament to our freedom.

SCIENTISM

"One must wait until the evening to see how splendid the day has been."

Sophocles

Formal Definition: Scientism is the belief that the scientific method is the only reliable way to gain knowledge about the world and that anything not scientifically proven is unworthy of consideration.

Now, let's dive into an analogy to make this concept more relatable. Imagine you're trying to solve a puzzle—a vast, intricate puzzle representing all the knowledge about the universe. Scientism would be like having only one type of tool, say a magnifying glass, and insisting that it's the only tool you need or trust to understand every piece of the puzzle.

In this analogy, the magnifying glass symbolizes the scientific method—careful observation, experimentation, and empirical evidence. It's an incredibly powerful tool, especially for understanding the tangible and measurable aspects of the puzzle, like the colors and shapes of the pieces. However, Scientism goes a step further, claiming that if you can't see something with the magnifying glass, it's either not real or not worth acknowledging.

To grasp this concept better, let's explore its implications. Imagine you encounter a piece of the puzzle that represents love, a complex and abstract emotion. Love is real, but it's not something you can dissect under a microscope or measure in a laboratory. According to Scientism, if you can't analyze it with the magnifying glass of science, then love might be dismissed as irrelevant or even non-existent.

Think about morality, too—the ideas of right and wrong. Scientism suggests that unless these concepts can be scientifically measured, they're merely subjective opinions without any real substance. It's like saying, "If I can't see it through my magnifying glass, it doesn't matter."

Now, let's expand the analogy to include different types of tools. Imagine the puzzle includes pieces that represent artistic expression, personal experiences, and spiritual beliefs. These aspects of human existence are like pieces that require different tools—a paintbrush, a diary, or a compass, for example.

Scientism insists that these tools are unnecessary or unreliable because they don't fit the scientific method. It implies that if you can't measure or observe something using the magnifying glass, it's not valuable knowledge. This approach, however, limits our understanding of the puzzle because it dismisses entire realms of human experience that are essential to a comprehensive understanding of life.

It's crucial to appreciate science and the magnifying glass for what they are—remarkable tools that excel at certain types of inquiries. However, embracing Scientism would be like trying to complete the puzzle with only one tool, neglecting the richness and diversity of human knowledge and experience.

Skepticism

"He who is not satisfied with a little is satisfied with nothing."

Epicurus

Skepticism is a philosophical idea that encourages you to doubt or question things until you have good reasons to believe in them.

Think of skepticism like being a scientist in your everyday life. Imagine you're a scientist investigating a new plant species you've never seen before. You wouldn't just immediately declare, "This plant has amazing properties!" No, you'd start by observing, testing, and collecting evidence.

Now, let's apply this idea to skepticism

Imagine you're in a magical forest filled with strange and colorful plants. Each plant claims to have a unique power: one promises to make you fly, another claims to grant you super strength, and a third says it can make you invisible. Sounds exciting, right?

Skepticism is like being the cautious scientist in this magical forest. Instead of plucking a leaf from the first plant and jumping off a cliff, you'd think, "Hold on, I need to be sure this plant can make me fly." So, you'd gather evidence. Maybe you'd watch someone else try it first to see if they fly safely.

When another plant boasts of its super strength, you wouldn't just rush to pick up a massive boulder. Instead, you'd conduct experiments. You might try lifting smaller rocks first to test the claim's validity.

And when you encounter the plant claiming to make you invisible, you wouldn't walk into a group of people thinking you're hidden. A good skeptic would consider, "Is there any proof this works? Let's investigate before believing."

Being skeptical is a bit like wearing a scientist's lab coat in your daily life. It means you don't accept claims or promises at face value. You seek evidence and test things before believing them, just like a scientist would.

Skepticism isn't about being negative or pessimistic. It's about being careful and thoughtful. It helps you avoid falling for things that may not be true or might even be harmful.

Solipsism

"I think I am, therefore, I am... I think."

George Carlin

Solipsism is a philosophical idea that suggests that only your mind is sure to exist, and everything else, including the external world and other people, might just be creations of your imagination.

Imagine you're in a dream. In this dream, you see people, places, and things, but you're the only one who truly exists in this dream world. Everyone and everything around you is a product of your mind, and when you wake up, they cease to exist. This is somewhat similar to the concept of solipsism.

Solipsism is like being the main character in your dream, where everything else is a creation of your imagination. In this dream, you might interact with other dream characters, talk to them, and even feel like they have their thoughts and feelings, just as you do in real life. But, according to solipsism, these dream characters are merely projections of your thoughts.

Now, let's dive a bit deeper into this idea.

In the world outside of solipsism, we believe that there is an objective reality—a reality that exists independently of our thoughts and feelings. For example, if you close your eyes and someone else is in the room, you believe that person still exists even when you can't see them. Solipsism challenges this belief.

Imagine you wake up from your dream, and everything in it disappears. The people, the places, and even the laws of physics that governed that dream world all vanished because they were products of your imagination. Solipsism suggests that our waking reality might be similar. According to this philosophy, the moment you stop thinking about something or someone, they cease to exist because they only exist in your mind.

But here's the catch: Solipsism is a very radical and controversial idea in philosophy. Most people don't believe in it because it raises some serious questions and challenges our common-sense understanding of the world.

For instance, if solipsism were true, how could we explain the experiences and thoughts of other people? In your dream, you might have conversations with dream characters, but those conversations are just different aspects of your thoughts. So, when you talk to your friend in the "real" world, is it just a conversation with yourself? It's a puzzling thought!

Moreover, if solipsism were accurate, how could we explain the unpredictability of the world? In your dream, everything happens because you imagined it that way, but in the real world, things often happen without your control. If everything is just a product of your mind, why can't you control everything that happens around you?

Sophism

"Always forgive, but never forget, else you will be a prisoner of your own hatred, and doomed to repeat your mistakes forever."

Wil Zeus

Sophism is a philosophical term that refers to a school of thought in ancient Greece, where individuals known as sophists were skilled in the art of persuasion and rhetoric. These thinkers were not concerned with absolute truth but rather focused on the ability to argue persuasively and win debates. Sophism arose during the 5th century BCE and played a significant role in the intellectual landscape of the time.

Imagine you're in a lively marketplace, surrounded by stalls selling various ideas instead of goods. In this philosophical marketplace, sophists are charismatic salespeople, adept at convincing you that their perspective is not only right but the only perspective worth considering. It's not about finding the ultimate truth; it's about skillfully presenting an argument that captivates and convinces.

Explaining Sophism: In the world of Sophism, the emphasis is on the art of persuasion rather than the pursuit of absolute truth. Picture a courtroom drama where two lawyers passionately present their cases, not necessarily to uncover an ultimate truth but to win the favor of the jury. Similarly, sophists were masters of rhetoric, the art of effective communication, and they believed that the ability to persuade was more valuable than discovering an objective reality.

Let's break down sophism further.

1. Persuasion over Truth: Sophists were like intellectual acrobats, skillfully navigating through arguments to sway opinions. It's akin to a debate club where winning is not about being right but about making the most compelling case. In the world of sophism, the journey of persuasion takes precedence over the destination of truth.

2. Relativity of Truth: Unlike other philosophical schools that sought universal truths, sophists believed that truth was subjective and could vary from person to person. Imagine if everyone in the marketplace had a different favorite fruit; for some, it's apples, for others, it's oranges. Similarly, for sophists, truth depended on individual perspectives and could change based on personal experiences and beliefs.

3. Rhetorical Mastery: Sophists were the wordsmiths of their time, using language as a powerful tool to shape opinions. Think of them as linguistic architects constructing intricate arguments. In our marketplace analogy, they are the eloquent storytellers who make you see the beauty in their version of the story, regardless of its objective accuracy.

4. **Pragmatism in Action:** Sophists were pragmatists, valuing the practical implications of an argument over its theoretical foundations. This is like choosing a smartphone based on its functionality rather than its underlying technology. Sophists were more concerned with the real-world impact of ideas and how they could be used effectively.

So, the next time you find yourself in a debate about any topic, be aware of the persuasive techniques at play. Embrace the Socratic spirit of seeking truth through thoughtful dialogue rather than being swayed solely by the artful words of a persuasive speaker.

Stoicism

"I am my world."

Ludwig Wittgenstein

Stoicism is a philosophy that teaches us how to find peace and strength in the face of life's challenges by controlling our emotions and focusing on what we can control.

Imagine a Ship on a Stormy Sea

Think of life as a vast ocean, and you are aboard a ship, sailing through it. Sometimes, the sea is calm, and other times, it gets stormy. Just like in life, sometimes everything goes smoothly, but there are moments of turbulence and challenges.

The Ship's Captain

In Stoicism, you are the captain of your ship. This means you are in charge of how you respond to what life throws at you. The captain doesn't control the weather, but they control how they navigate through it.

The Stoic Toolbox

Emotion Control: Stoicism teaches you to manage your emotions. Imagine the stormy sea as your emotions run wild. A Stoic captain doesn't let these emotional storms sink their ship. They learn to stay calm and collected.

Focus on What You Can Control: The Stoic captain doesn't waste energy on things they can't control, like the weather. Instead, they concentrate on the ship's sails, rudder, and crew. In life, this means focusing on your actions, thoughts, and decisions.

Acceptance: Storms are part of the sea's nature, just like challenges are part of life's nature. Stoicism encourages you to accept that storms will come, and it's your reaction that matters. Instead of complaining about the storm, the Stoic captain prepares and adapts.

An Example of Stoicism

Imagine you have an important test coming up. It's natural to feel anxious – that's the storm on your emotional sea. But a Stoic captain would acknowledge their anxiety and then focus on what they can control. They might start studying, get a good night's sleep, and eat a healthy meal. They understand that worrying about the difficulty of the test or what others think is beyond their control, so they let go of those concerns. When the day of the test arrives, they've done everything they can. If the test is challenging, they accept it as part of life's storms. Instead of getting upset, they maintain their composure, knowing that they did their best.

The Stoic Mindset

Stoicism isn't about suppressing emotions or pretending to be tough. It's about acknowledging your feelings while choosing how to respond wisely. Just like a good captain, you steer your ship through life's ups and downs.

Benefits of Stoicism

Inner Peace: By controlling your reactions, you can find calmness amid chaos.

Resilience: Stoicism helps you bounce back from setbacks, just like a ship riding out a storm.

Improved Decision-Making: When you focus on what you can control, you make better choices.

Happier Relationships: Stoicism encourages empathy and understanding toward others.

Less Stress: By not worrying about what's beyond your control, you reduce stress.

Stoicism reminds us that while we can't control everything that happens, we have the power to choose how we respond. It's a philosophy that empowers you to find inner strength, face challenges with resilience, and sail through life's storms with grace. So, when the waves of life get rough, remember your Stoic captain's hat and steer your ship towards serenity and strength.

STRUCTURALISM

"What a waste my life would be without all the beautiful mistakes I've made."

Alice Bag

Structuralism is a fancy term in philosophy that helps us understand how we make sense of the world around us. Imagine you have a puzzle—a big, complicated one with lots of pieces. Each puzzle piece on its own might not make much sense, but when you put it together just right, it creates a beautiful picture.

Now, let's apply this idea to structuralism. In philosophy, structuralism is like trying to understand the big picture by studying the individual pieces that make it up. Instead of looking at something as a whole, structuralists break it down into its smaller parts to figure out how they connect and work together to create meaning.

Here's a formal definition: Structuralism is a way of thinking that focuses on the relationships and patterns between smaller elements to understand the larger system or structure.

Imagine you're reading a book. Structuralism would encourage you to look at how each word, sentence, and paragraph fits together. It's not just about reading the story; it's about understanding how the language and the author's choices create the story's meaning.

To help you grasp this idea better, think of a language as another example of structuralism. Language isn't just a bunch of random words thrown together; it follows a structure with grammar rules. Those rules help us communicate effectively. If you start mixing up words and grammar, the meaning can get all jumbled up. Structuralists study these rules and patterns to understand how language works as a whole.

Now, let's take it a step further. Imagine you're trying to understand society. Structuralism helps you look at the various parts of society—like family, education, and government—and how they connect. It's not just about studying each part individually; it's about figuring out how they interact to create the social structure we live in.

Think of society as a giant puzzle. Each part, like a family or a school, has its unique characteristics and rules. Structuralism asks, "How do these different pieces fit together to form our society?" It's like looking at all the puzzle pieces and finding the connections between them to reveal the bigger picture.

But here's where it gets interesting: structuralism doesn't stop at puzzles or language or society. It can be applied to almost anything! Art, music, culture, even your thoughts and feelings—structuralism helps us see how the smaller elements come together to create meaning and understanding.

Let's talk about art. An artist doesn't just throw colors randomly onto a canvas. They use lines, shapes, and colors in a structured way to convey emotions and ideas.

Structuralism looks at how these elements work together to create the overall artistic experience.

Social contract theory

"This place is a dream. Only a sleeper considers it real. Then death comes like dawn, and you wake up laughing at what you thought was your grief."

Rumi

Social contract theory is a philosophical idea that helps us understand how societies form and function. It suggests that people come together and agree on rules and a government to protect their rights and maintain order in exchange for giving up some of their freedom.

Imagine you and a group of friends decide to play a game. But before you start, you need to set some rules. Each person has their ideas about how the game should be played, and there's a chance that without rules, the game could become chaotic and not much fun. So, you all gather around and agree on a set of rules to make the game fair and enjoyable for everyone. These rules are like the social contract.

Explanation

Social contract theory is like setting rules for a game, but instead of a game, it's about how a whole society works. Let's break it down into simpler terms:

People and Freedom: In any society, people have individual freedoms. These are like your personal choices and actions, such as what you wear, eat, or say. You can think of these freedoms as your playing abilities in the game.

The Need for Order: Just like in our game example, societies also need some order to function smoothly. Without any rules, there could be chaos and conflicts. For instance, without traffic rules, driving would be dangerous.

Creating the Social Contract: So, what do people do? They come together and agree on a set of rules and a government to enforce those rules. This agreement is a social contract. In our game analogy, it's like everyone sitting down and deciding the rules of the game together.

Giving up Some Freedom: Here's the tricky part: in exchange for this order and protection, people have to give up some of their freedoms. Just like in the game, where you follow the rules even if they limit your actions a bit, in society, you obey laws and rules that restrict certain behaviors.

Benefits of the Social Contract: But why would anyone agree to give up some of their freedom? Well, because the social contract offers important benefits. In our game, the rules make sure the game is fair and everyone has a chance to win. In society, the social contract ensures safety, protection of property, and a fair system for resolving disputes.

Role of Government: The government is like the referee in our game. It's there to make sure everyone follows the rules (laws) and to protect people's rights. If someone breaks the rules, the government steps in, just like a referee would in a game if someone cheats.

Consent and Ongoing Agreement: Importantly, the social contract relies on the idea of consent. People agree to this contract willingly, and they can change the rules (laws) if they want through a democratic process, like voting for new leaders or passing new laws.

So, It's a way for people to live together peacefully, respecting each other's rights, and creating a society where everyone has a chance to thrive.

STRUCTURAL FUNCTIONALISM

"Mother used to say that however miserable one is, there's always something to be thankful for. And each morning, when the sky brightened and light began to flood my cell, I agreed with her."

Albert Camus

Structural Functionalism is a sociological perspective that views society as a complex system with interconnected parts, each serving a specific function to maintain the overall stability and equilibrium of the social order.

In simpler terms, think of society as a giant puzzle, where each puzzle piece represents a different part of the whole. Now, imagine that these puzzle pieces work together like a well-coordinated team to make the entire picture complete and functional. This is essentially what Structural Functionalism is all about – understanding how the various parts of society, like education, family, government, and economy, fit together and contribute to the smooth functioning of the overall social system.

Let's break it down further with a relatable analogy. Picture a school. In this school, there are students, teachers, administrators, janitors, and other staff members. Now, each of these individuals has a specific role or function within the school system. Students learn, teachers educate, administrators manage, janitors clean, and so on. Just like the puzzle pieces, these roles fit together to create a functioning school environment.

Now, let's think about what happens if one of these roles isn't fulfilled. If the teachers suddenly stop teaching, chaos will ensue. Students wouldn't learn, and the entire purpose of the school – education – would be compromised. This disruption would affect not only the students but also the administrators, janitors, and other staff members whose functions depend on the smooth operation of the educational system.

This is where the idea of "function" comes into play in Structural Functionalism. Each part of society, or each role in our school analogy, has a specific function or purpose. These functions contribute to the overall stability and balance of the social system. When everything works as it should, society functions smoothly, just like a well-put-together puzzle or a smoothly-running school.

However, it's important to note that Structural Functionalism doesn't just focus on the positive aspects of society. It also acknowledges that there can be dysfunctions – things that disrupt the smooth operation of the social system. Going back to our school analogy, a dysfunction could be a conflict between teachers and administrators, leading to a breakdown in communication and cooperation.

In conclusion, Structural Functionalism is like looking at society as a giant, interconnected puzzle where each piece has a specific role to play. The smooth functioning of society depends on these parts working together harmoniously, much like the various roles in a school.

This perspective helps us understand how different aspects of society contribute to its overall stability and, at the same time, how disruptions or dysfunctions can impact the social order. So, the next time you're in school or any social setting, think about how each person and each role plays a crucial part in the larger picture of society.

Subjectivism

"Until the day when God shall deign to reveal the future to man, all human wisdom is summed up in these two words,-Wait and hope."

Alexandre Dumas

Subjectivism is a philosophical term that refers to the idea that reality is, to a large extent, shaped by individual perspectives and experiences. In simpler terms, it suggests that what we perceive and believe is influenced by our personal feelings, thoughts, and interpretations. Subjectivism places a strong emphasis on the role of the subject, or the individual, in shaping their own understanding of the world.

Formal Definition: Subjectivism is a philosophical perspective asserting that reality is fundamentally dependent on individual subjectivity, emphasizing the role of personal feelings, beliefs, and interpretations in shaping one's understanding of the world.

Analogy

The Art Gallery of Perception

Imagine you are in an art gallery filled with various paintings, each unique and open to interpretation. In this gallery, every visitor sees the artwork differently based on their personal experiences, emotions, and preferences. This diversity of perspectives reflects the essence of subjectivism.

Now, let's delve deeper into the concept.

Explaining Subjectivism

Subjectivism challenges the idea that there is an objective, universal truth that applies to everyone. Instead, it suggests that truth is a subjective experience, varying from person to person. To illustrate this, consider the following analogy of watching a movie.

Imagine a group of friends watching a movie together. Each person brings their background, emotions, and past experiences to the viewing. As the film unfolds, some may find it funny, others might see it as sad, and a few could interpret it as thrilling. The movie itself remains unchanged, but each person's subjective experience of it is unique.

In the realm of philosophy, subjectivism applies this idea to broader aspects of life. It asserts that our perceptions of reality, morality, and knowledge are influenced by our subjectivity. What we consider right or wrong, beautiful or ugly, true or false, is shaped by our perspectives.

Everyday Examples of Subjectivism

Taste in Music: Different people enjoy different genres of music. While one person may find joy in classical melodies, another might prefer the energetic beats of hip-hop. Subjectivism explains these preferences by highlighting the role of personal taste and individual experiences.

Moral Values: Subjectivism is particularly relevant in discussions about morality. For example, the perception of what is morally right or wrong can vary from person to person based on their cultural background, upbringing, and personal beliefs.

Beauty Standards: Consider the concept of beauty. What one person finds aesthetically pleasing may not align with someone else's definition of beauty. Subjectivism suggests that our perceptions of beauty are influenced by our unique experiences and cultural influences.

In essence, subjectivism encourages us to recognize and appreciate the diversity of human perspectives. It invites us to understand that each person's viewpoint is valid in their context, fostering a more open-minded and empathetic approach to the rich tapestry of human experience. Just as the movie of reality unfolds differently for each viewer in our analogy, subjectivism teaches us to acknowledge and respect the varied interpretations that shape our understanding of the world.

Transcendentalism

"Every man is a creature of the age in which he lives and few are able to raise themselves above the ideas of the time."

Voltaire

Transcendentalism is a philosophical movement that emerged in the 19th century in the United States. At its core, it is the belief in the inherent goodness of people and nature, emphasizing the importance of individual intuition, self-reliance, and the connection between the human spirit and the natural world.

Formal Definition: Transcendentalism is a philosophical and literary movement that emerged in the 1830s and 1840s, primarily in the New England region of the United States. It emphasizes the inherent goodness of people and nature, advocating for the individual's ability to connect with the divine through intuition and personal experience. Transcendentalists reject societal conformity and stress the importance of self-reliance and the spiritual connection with the natural world.

Imagine life as a grand symphony, with each person playing a unique instrument, contributing to the harmonious melody of existence. Transcendentalism is like a musical conductor guiding this symphony, encouraging each instrument to play its part authentically and in harmony with the others.

In this analogy, the instruments represent individuals, each with their inherent goodness and unique qualities. The conductor symbolizes the transcendent force, an unseen energy that connects and unifies all the instruments – the divine presence that Transcendentalists believe exists within and around us.

Individual Instruments

Inherent Goodness and Self-Reliance

Just as each instrument in a symphony has its unique sound and role, Transcendentalism celebrates the inherent goodness within each person. It asserts that individuals are born with a natural inclination towards goodness, and through self-discovery and self-reliance, they can express their virtuous nature.

Picture a violin representing an individual. The strings resonate with the inherent goodness, and as the player – the individual – learns to tune and play the instrument, the beautiful melody of their authentic self emerges. Transcendentalists encourage people to listen to their inner music, to trust their intuition, and to be confident in their ability to navigate the score of life.

The Conductor

Nature and Intuition

In the symphony of life, nature is the conductor guiding the musicians. The rustle of leaves, the flow of rivers, and the song of birds all contribute to the overarching composition of existence. Transcendentalists believe that by immersing oneself in nature, individuals can better understand the rhythm of life and connect with the divine.

Imagine standing in a lush forest, surrounded by towering trees and the gentle sounds of a babbling brook. This natural setting serves as a metaphorical conductor, orchestrating a symphony of sensations that speak to the soul. Intuition, represented by the conductor, becomes the guide, leading individuals to a deeper understanding of themselves and their connection to the larger cosmic orchestra.

In the grand symphony of Transcendentalism, diversity is celebrated, and harmony arises from the authentic expression of each instrument. The movement encourages young minds to embrace their unique qualities, trust their inner wisdom, and cultivate a profound connection with the natural world. Just as a symphony is enriched by the variety of instruments playing in unity, Transcendentalism teaches that embracing our goodness and tuning into the rhythm of nature can create a beautiful and harmonious life symphony.

Thank you so much for choosing my book! Your thoughts mean a lot to me, and if you could spare a few minutes, I'd greatly appreciate your review on Amazon – it would be incredibly helpful! I've also attached a curated list of 100 philosophy books to enhance your knowledge.

Feel free to reach out for discussions via email at daniel.chechick@gmail.com or connect on Instagram: @existential.reflections

Your engagement is truly valued!

Further Readings

Existentialism

Beckett, Samuel: Waiting for Godot (1953)

Camus, Albert: The Stranger (1942)

Camus, Albert: The Myth of Sisyphus (1942)

Camus, Albert: The Plague (1947)

Camus, Albert: The Rebel (1951)

Camus, Albert: The Fall (1956)

Camus, Albert: A Happy Death (1971)

Camus, Albert: The First Man (1994)

Dostoevsky, Fyodor: Notes from the Underground (1864)

Dostoevsky, Fyodor: Crime and Punishment (1866)

Dostoevsky, Fyodor: The Idiot (1869)

Dostoevsky, Fyodor: Demons (1872)

Dostoevsky, Fyodor: The Brothers Karamazov (1880)

Heidegger, Martin: Being and Time (1927)

Heidegger, Martin: The Question concerning Technology (1954)

Kafka, Franz: The Metamorphosis (1915)

Kafka, Franz: The Trial (1925)

Kafka, Franz: The Castle (1926)

Kierkegaard, Søren: Either/Or (1843)

Kierkegaard, Søren: Fear and Trembling (1843)

Kierkegaard, Søren: The Concept of Anxiety (1844)

Kierkegaard, Søren: Stages on Life's Way (1845)

Kierkegaard, Søren: Works of Love (1847)

Kierkegaard, Søren: The Sickness unto Death (1849)

Kierkegaard, Søren: The Lily of the Field and the Bird of the Air (1849)

Nietzsche, Friedrich: The Birth of Tragedy (1872)

Nietzsche, Friedrich: Human, All Too Human (1878)

Nietzsche, Friedrich: The Dawn of Day (1881)

Nietzsche, Friedrich: The Gay Science (1882)

Nietzsche, Friedrich: Thus Spoke Zarathustra (1883)

Nietzsche, Friedrich: Beyond Good and Evil (1886)

Nietzsche, Friedrich: On the Genealogy of Morals (1887)

Nietzsche, Friedrich: Twilight of the Idols and The Antichrist (1888)

Sartre, Jean-Paul: Existentialism is a Humanism (1946)

Sartre, Jean-Paul: Nausea (1938)

Sartre, Jean-Paul: The Wall (1939) and Other Stories

Sartre, Jean-Paul: Being and Nothingness (1943)

Sartre, Jean-Paul: No Exit (1944) and Three Other Plays

Stoicism

Aurelius, Marcus: Meditations (180 AD)

Epictetus: Discourses and Selected Writings (108 AD)

Epictetus: The Enchiridion (125 AD)

Seneca: On the Shortness of Life (49 AD)

Seneca: Letters from a Stoic (65 AD)

Psychology

    Frankl, Viktor: Man's Search for Meaning (1946)

    Freud, Sigmund: The Interpretation of Dreams (1899)

    Freud, Sigmund: The Future Of Illusion (1989)

    Jung, Carl: Memories, Dreams, Reflections (1961)

    Jung, Carl: Man and His Symbols (1964)

    Jung, Carl: Two Essays on Analytical Psychology – C.W. Vol.7 (1967)

    Jung, Carl: Symbols of Transformation – C.W. Vol.5 (1967)

    Jung, Carl: Psychology & Alchemy – C.W. Vol.12 (1968)

    Jung, Carl: The Archetypes and The Collective Unconscious – Collected Works Vol.9 Part 1 (1969)

    Jung, Carl: Aion: Researches into the Phenomenology of the Self – C.W. Vol.9 Part 2 (1969)

    Jung, Carl: Mysterium Coniunctionis – C.W. Vol.14 (1970)

    Jung, Carl: Psychological Types – C.W. Vol.6 (1971)

    Jung, Carl: Modern Man In Search of a Soul (1933)

Eastern philosophy

    Confucius: The Analects (2th century BC)

    Hesse, Hermann: Siddhartha (1922)

    Musashi, Miyamoto: The Book of Five Rings (1643)

    Tzu, Lao: Tao Te Ching (6th century BC)

    Tzu, Sun: The Art of War (5th century BC)

    Watts, Alan: The Way of Zen (1957)

Watts, Alan: Tao – The Watercourse Way (1975)

Yogananda, Paramahansa: Autobiography of a Yogi (1946)

Zhou, Zhuang: The Book of Chuang Tzu (4th – 2th century BC)

Unknown author: The Bhagavad Gita (2nd century BC)

Unknown author: The Upanishads (7th – 5th century BC)

Unknown author: The Dhammapada (5th – 4th century BC)

The Classics

Alighieri, Dante: The Divine Comedy (1321)

Austen, Jane: Pride and Prejudice (1813)

Bradbury, Ray: Fahrenheit 451 (1953)

Carroll, Lewis: Alice's Adventures in Wonderland (1865)

Cervantes, Miguel de: Don Quixote (1615)

Dickens, Charles: Great Expectations (1860)

Frank, Anne: The Diary of a Young Girl (1947)

Faulkner, William: The Sound and the Fury (1929)

Fitzgerald, F. Scott: The Great Gatsby (1925)

Goethe, Johann Wolfgang von: Faust (1829)

Golding, William: Lord of the Flies (1954)

Heller, Joseph: Catch-22 (1961)

Herbert, Frank: Dune (1965)

Homer: The Iliad (7th century BC)

Homer: The Odyssey (7th century BC)

Huxley, Aldous: Brave New World (1932)

Joyce, James: *Ulysses* (1922)

Lee, Harper: *To Kill a Mockingbird* (1960)

Machiavelli, Niccolò: *The Prince* (1532)

Márquez, Gabriel García: *One Hundred Years of Solitude* (1967)

Melville, Herman: *Moby Dick* (1851)

Milton, John: *Paradise Lost* (1667)

Orwell, George: *Animal Farm* (1945)

Orwell, George: *Nineteen Eighty-Four* (1949)

Proust, Marcel: *In Search of Lost Time* (1913)

Salinger, J.D: *The Catcher in the Rye* (1951)

Shakespeare, William: *Hamlet* (1609)

Shelley, Mary: *Frankenstein* (1823)

Solzhenitsyn, Aleksandr: *The Gulag Archipielago* (1974)

Steinbeck, John: *The Grapes of Wrath* (1939)

Stoker, Bram: *Dracula* (1897)

Tolstoy, Leo: *War and Peace* (1869)

Tolstoy, Leo: *Anna Karenina* (1878)

Tolstoy, Leo: *The Death Of Ivan Ilich* (1886)

Vonnegut, Kurt: *Slaughterhouse-Five* (1969)

Woolf, Virginia: *To the Lighthouse* (1927)

Twain, Mark: *The Adventures of Huckleberry Finn* (1844)